AMBUSHED!

THE ASSASSINATION PLOT AGAINST PRESIDENT GARFIELD

MEDICAL FIASCOES SERIES

AMBUSHED!

THE ASSASSINATION PLOT AGAINST PRESIDENT GARFIELD

GAIL JARROW

SIBERT HONOR WINNER

CALKINS CREEK

AN IMPRINT OF ASTRA BOOKS FOR YOUNG READERS

New York

For information about permission to reproduce selections from this book, please contact permissions@astrapublishinghouse.com.

Calkins Creek
An imprint of Astra Books for Young Readers, a division of Astra Publishing House
astrapublishinghouse.com
Printed in China

ISBN: 978-1-68437-814-2 (hc)
ISBN: 978-1-63592-463-3 (eBook)
Library of Congress Control Number: 2020947627

First edition
10 9 8 7 6 5 4 3 2

Design by Red Herring Design
The text is set in Chaparral.
The titles are set in Knockout and Sharp Grotesk.

CONTENTS

President James A. Garfield

For Petra —May you face a world with fewer medical fiascoes.

View of Pennsylvania Avenue and the
U.S. Capitol, Washington, DC, in 1880

CHAPTER ONE
WASHINGTON, 1881

N O ONE NOTICED THE SCRAWNY MAN IN A SHABBY COAT LURKING in the doorway shadows. No one realized what was happening at the moment he stepped out and approached the gentleman wearing the fine, gray suit.

On a warm summer day in 1881, the lives of these two men became violently—and forever—intertwined.

Charles and James had in common one of life's most difficult challenges. Both lost a parent at a young age. But while Charles always felt alienated and alone, James grew up surrounded by loving family and friends.

As young men, both developed deep religious beliefs. Yet their faith took them in very different directions.

Charles imagined himself to be clever, handsome, and competent. Few people who knew him agreed with that assessment. Convinced he was destined for greatness, Charles always chose the easiest path possible, which brought failure at almost everything he did.

James was blessed with intelligence, good looks, and the willingness to work hard. These traits led to significant accomplishments. His success was the reason Charles hunted him down.

For weeks, Charles had planned the attack. In his pocket he carried a letter explaining why he was forced to act. He expected all Americans to thank him for saving the nation.

Taking a deep breath, Charles raised his ivory-handled pistol and aimed at James's back.

What happened next changed history and resulted in one of America's most tragic medical fiascoes.

Garfield's birthplace and childhood home (above). He was the last U.S. president to be born in a log cabin. James as a teen on the *Evening Star* canal boat, which transported products and supplies between Cleveland and Pittsburgh. These illustrations were included in an 1881 Garfield biography.

CHAPTER TWO
LOG CABIN BOY

"There is one country on the globe where a boy
need not be born on the steps of the throne or in
the seats of wealth to rise to distinguished place."

—B. A. Hinsdale, Garfield friend and biographer

WHEN JAMES ABRAM GARFIELD RAN FOR POLITICAL OFFICE, HIS supporters told voters that he had been born in a log cabin and worked his way from poverty to admirable achievements. The campaign's strategy was to show that he was an honorable, talented man who understood the struggles of ordinary Americans. Other candidates had tried the log cabin tactic, too. In Garfield's case, the story was true.

He was born on November 19, 1831, in his parents' log house in northeastern Ohio. A big baby weighing ten pounds, James joined a brother and two sisters. His parents named him after another son who had died as a toddler two years before. Abram and Eliza Garfield farmed their land in sparsely populated Orange Township, not far from Lake Erie and Cleveland. They barely managed to support their young family.

When James was eighteen months old, a fast-burning fire spread in the nearby woods.

For hours, his father desperately worked to save the farm, chopping away brush and digging ditches. Abram stopped the flames, though the exertion sapped his strength. He fell ill, likely from pneumonia, and never recovered. Soon after the fire, Abram died at age thirty-three.

James's uncle and aunt lived on the adjacent property, and they did what they could to help Eliza manage her land. The Garfield children pitched in. But life was difficult for a farm family without a father. Eliza was proud of the fact that, through hard work, they paid all their debts and received no charity.

A NEW PATH

At age three, James began attending the local schoolhouse with his siblings, often riding there on his brother's back. The little boy had an excellent memory and enjoyed school. Whenever James was able to get his hands on a book—and there weren't many around—he read it over and over. Later in life, he described having a "hunger and thirst for knowledge."

As he grew older, James helped with the farm work and took odd jobs to support the family. Hiring himself out to neighbors and relatives, he chopped wood, plowed fields, brought in hay, and built barns and cabins. His mother later said that James "was never still a minute at a time in his whole life."

By fifteen, he had grown tall and strong and felt ready to make his way in the world. Enchanted by the boats on Lake Erie and novels about the sea, James decided to become a sailor.

During the summer of 1848, at the age of sixteen, James went to work on his older cousin's boat on the canal that connected Cleveland and Pittsburgh, Pennsylvania. The canal wasn't the sea, but James considered his new job the first step toward reaching his goal.

At fourteen dollars a month, his duties included controlling the mules along the canal's towpath as they pulled the boat, which was loaded with supplies such as lumber, coal, iron, or copper ore. James didn't know how to

1848 April

4 Sun rained A.M. chopped P.M.
5 ... chopped to day quite warm
6 Thur chopped wood to day raining
7 Frid worked for Marenus A.M. to Dutchmans for...
8 Sat split wood A.M. piled wood P.M Marenus marked...
9 Sun went over to pike then to the burgh back to... wood
10 Mon worked for Edward Barns. chopped wood
11 Tues worked for Barns very very warm
12 Wend worked for Barns rained some
13 Thur worked for Barns warm
14 Frid worked for Barns spit snow a little P.M.
15 Sat worked for Barns half day. to Halbs
16 Sun went to the Canal very warm
17 Mon worked for Barns very warm
18 Tues worked for Barns chopping
19 Wedn worked for Barns
20 Thur worked for Barns sawing
21 Frid worked for Barns chopping warm
22 Sat worked for Barns. chopping warm
23 Sun went to uncle J. Garfield

At age sixteen James began a diary, which he continued throughout his life. In his entries for April 1848, he recorded the weather and the odd jobs he did each day to help support his mother: chopping, splitting, piling, and sawing wood (highlighted above).

swim, and whenever he tumbled into the canal—more than a dozen times by his count—someone had to pull him out.

After less than seven weeks, however, James's plans fell apart when he developed the chills and fevers of malaria. Too sick to work, he was forced to go home to his mother for nursing. For three months James endured the symptoms, feeling so weak that he had to stay in bed part of the time. For another two months he didn't have the strength and stamina to do any of the strenuous physical labor his previous jobs required.

James intended to return to the canal as soon as he was strong enough. His mother had other ideas. Eliza Garfield recognized her son's intellectual curiosity, and she encouraged him to get more instruction than had been offered at the local schoolhouse. She handed him seventeen dollars that she and his brother had saved for James's education.

Garfield's mother, Eliza (1801–1888), encouraged her son to get an education.

In March 1849, James followed her advice. Along with two friends, he headed about ten miles away to Geauga Seminary, a school of 250 students run by the Free Will Baptist religious denomination. The curriculum included grammar, mental arithmetic, philosophy, geography, and algebra. James did well in his studies. He was one of only three algebra students to finish the course. The other fifteen dropped out, unable to understand the math.

James discovered that seventeen dollars wasn't enough to cover his tuition, room, and meals. To earn more, he did carpentry work on Saturdays. That winter he found a job teaching at a small community school for twelve dollars a month.

Barely eighteen, James was not much older than some of his students, and he had trouble controlling the unruly ones. But he needed the income, and he stuck with it. Six days before his eighteenth birthday, he wrote in his diary, "Punished S. Herrington severely for disobeying and being saucy. [H]e endeavored to fight me but he finally gave up and is now a good boy." Off and on for a couple of years, James earned money for his spring and fall terms by teaching in country schools during the winter.

By this time, his goal had shifted from sailing to educating himself. He intended to make his living using his mind, not his back and hands. James never regretted going to school instead of staying on the canal. In fact, he felt lucky. "By the providence of God I am what I am, and not a sailor," he wrote a month before he turned nineteen. "I Thank Him."

REACHING HIGHER

In late summer 1851, James enrolled at a new co-educational school started by the Disciples of Christ, the Protestant church of his parents. Western Reserve Eclectic Institute (called Hiram College after 1867) was in Hiram, Ohio, about twenty-five miles from his mother's home. The college had a more extensive and challenging curriculum than did the one at Geauga Seminary.

James grew to six feet and had light-blue eyes. While a student at Western Reserve Eclectic Institute, he made a habit of learning twelve new words every day.

To pay for his tuition and expenses, James worked as a carpenter and as the school's janitor. He became so proficient in his studies that, even before he graduated, he was hired to teach classes in Greek, Latin, algebra, and penmanship.

James's religious beliefs were central to his life. While a student at the Eclectic Institute, he traveled to area Disciples of Christ churches, where he was paid to give Sunday sermons.

He valued his two years at the Eclectic along with the close friends he had made, including his future wife, Lucretia (Crete) Rudolph. But to reach great success in the world, James knew he needed a more rigorous college education.

After corresponding with the heads of several colleges, he decided to attend Williams College, a small, all-male school in the hills of northwestern Massachusetts. He believed that a New England college would best broaden his mind by exposing him to a range of ideas and viewpoints. He expected the professors and students there to have opinions about politics, religion, and literature beyond what he'd experienced in Ohio.

It was a brave step for the twenty-two-year-old. For the first time, he would leave his mother, older brother and two sisters, and many other close relatives. He'd miss the friends he'd known all his life, but he hoped to make new ones.

In the summer of 1854, James journeyed to Williams College. Based on his performance on entrance tests, he was accepted as a junior. He soon realized that his fellow students had received better preparation for college, though he was determined to surpass them. "If I am blessed with life and health," he wrote in his diary, "I will stand at least among the first in that class."

At Williams, James took advantage of his new opportunities. "There are 25000 books in the libraries here within a few feet of me," he wrote his mother, "so I can have all the books to read I want."

James studied numerous subjects for the first time, including chemistry, economics, and German. He joined a literary society and the editorial board of the college magazine. His gregarious nature and sense of humor earned him friends. His strong public-speaking skills, developed from preaching and teaching, earned him respect as an excellent debater.

A former Williams student later wrote that James was "one of the greatest natural debaters ever seen at Williams College." As a speaker, he was popular among faculty, students, and townspeople. "His massive figure, commanding, self-confident manner, and magnificent bursts of fiery eloquence, won and held the attention of his audience from the moment he opened his lips."

James didn't leave behind his religious beliefs. He visited Disciples of Christ meetings in neighboring Vermont and New York, often preaching for money to pay his college expenses.

In August 1856, after two years, James earned his bachelor of arts degree and graduated with honors. The close ties he formed at Williams College would last the rest of his life.

James and Lucretia in their engagement photograph. The two married on November 11, 1858. Lucretia (Crete) Rudolph Garfield (1832–1918) met her future husband at the Geauga Seminary, where they both were students. They later attended the Eclectic Institute together and were both members of the Disciples of Christ church. Like James, Lucretia loved literature and valued education. After graduating from the Eclectic and before marrying, she taught schoolchildren in Cleveland and smaller Ohio communities.

FRESH AMBITIONS

Officials at the Eclectic Institute asked their former student to return to Hiram as a teacher. Garfield reluctantly agreed to come back for just one year. But when the school's president was later ousted for incompetence, the trustees appointed Garfield to the position. The single year turned into five.

Now that he was responsible for the education of more than 200 students, Garfield improved the academic curriculum. Besides serving as president, he also taught Greek, Latin, mathematics, geology, English literature, history, grammar, and philosophy.

In his private life, Garfield finally married Lucretia Rudolph in November 1858, after several years of courtship. They moved into a house in Hiram, close to the school.

James Garfield became known for his leadership at the Eclectic Institute and for his continued preaching throughout the area. In August 1859, the local Republican Party asked him to run for Ohio State Senate. Garfield jumped at the offer. Now twenty-seven, he was too ambitious to remain forever a teacher or even the head of a school. "I have for some years had it in contemplation to enter the field of statesmanship," he wrote in his diary, ". . . and if this plan succeeds I shall have gained a step in the direction of my purpose."

The plan succeeded, and Garfield won his first political office. Because his Ohio Senate duties weren't full-time, he continued as president and teacher at the Eclectic Institute, too. As if that weren't enough to keep him busy, Garfield decided to study law with guidance from attorneys at a Cleveland law firm. In early 1861, Garfield was admitted to the bar. Although he was now permitted to practice law in Ohio, he didn't have the chance.

A war got in the way.

THE CIVIL WAR

The Battle of Chickamauga, as depicted in this 1890 print, was fought in Georgia on September 18–20, 1863. It was one of the bloodiest of the entire war. Union soldiers wear blue uniforms, and Confederates are in gray. During this battle, which the Confederates won, James Garfield served as chief of staff to Union general William Rosecrans.

For decades, the northern and southern regions of the United States bitterly argued over slavery. While states in the North abolished it, the South considered slave labor to be essential to its economic success. As the country expanded westward, the argument intensified: When new states and territories were added to the nation, should slavery be permitted in them?

The 1860 election of Republican Abraham Lincoln as president was the last straw for the South because he opposed allowing slavery in these western areas. Eleven southern states seceded from the United States, forming the Confederate States of America. On April 12, 1861, Confederate cannons in Charleston, South Carolina, fired on the U.S. garrison at Fort Sumter in the harbor. The Civil War had begun.

The seceding Confederate states fought for their independence. The remaining states led by Lincoln (the Union) battled to end the rebellion. By the time the four-year conflict ended, four million men had taken up weapons. An estimated 620,000 to 750,000 of them died.

James Garfield in uniform. After his wartime service ended, his wife, friends, and family continued to refer to him as "The General."

WAR DRUMS

While 1860 was a happy year for the Garfields because their first child, Eliza (nicknamed Trot), was born that July, it was a turbulent year for the nation.

After Abraham Lincoln was elected president in November, rumbles of rebellion swept the southern states. The Confederate states chose to secede from the United States rather than let the federal government, led by Lincoln, limit slavery.

Like many people in his corner of Ohio, Garfield had long opposed slavery. In October 1857, he gave money to a runaway slave passing through Hiram on his way from Kentucky to freedom in Canada. Later that month, Garfield wrote in his diary, "Slavery has had its day, or at any rate is fast having it."

After the Confederate attack on Fort Sumter, Garfield grasped what the future held. He wrote Lucretia from Columbus, where the Ohio Senate was in session: "I can see nothing now before us but a long and sanguinary war." Yet no matter how bloody the war might prove to be, he felt the obligation to join the fight "to stand by the country and sustain its authority."

Giving up his obligations at the Eclectic and leaving Lucretia and Trot to move in with her parents in Hiram, Garfield went to war. In August 1861, he became a colonel in the Union army, taking charge of a regiment of about a thousand Ohio soldiers, some of whom were students from the Eclectic Institute.

Garfield learned about military leadership through experience and observation of the professional soldiers around him. As the Confederates attempted to take control of Kentucky, a border state between North and South, Garfield was assigned to help push them out. He was successful. He later participated in military campaigns by the Union army to defeat the Confederates in Tennessee, Georgia, Mississippi, and Alabama.

While marching through Alabama in June 1862, Garfield got a disturbing look at slavery on southern plantations. "No one who sees the splendor and luxury of these wealthy planters' homes," he wrote his wife, "can fail to see that the 'Peculiar Institution' has great claims for the rich and yet no one can fail to see that it is the poor man's bane."

In September 1862, President Lincoln issued the Preliminary Emancipation Proclamation, declaring freedom for slaves in the Confederate states as of January 1, 1863. This meant that the Union's goal would be to abolish slavery as well as to suppress the southern states' rebellion. Pleased, Garfield wrote to Lucretia, "The President's head is right, God grant he may have the strength to stand up to his convictions and carry them to the full."

DISEASE STRIKES

Garfield hated watching men die from wounds, but the greatest killer of the Civil War was sickness. "This fighting with disease," he wrote Lucretia, "is infinitely more horrible than battle."

In the 1860s, doctors hadn't yet learned that microbes cause disease. They didn't realize that airborne viruses and bacteria led to pneumonia, measles, and smallpox among soldiers living in crowded conditions. The medical community didn't know that microorganisms transmitted by mosquitoes, which thrive in wet areas, produce malaria. No one understood that microbes in body waste contaminated drinking water and caused dysentery and typhoid fever.

Disease brought down Garfield, too. He went through several bouts of dysentery. In the summer of 1862, he suffered from fever, diarrhea, extreme fatigue, and jaundice, losing more than forty pounds. Although his illness wasn't diagnosed, he called it camp fever, a term often used for typhoid fever. Barely able to walk, Garfield returned home to Hiram to recover. The only effective treatment then was rest, with the hope that the body would fight the infection.

Meanwhile, Garfield's Ohio political friends had been working toward winning him a seat in the U.S. Congress. In the fall of 1862, without any campaigning on his part, Garfield was elected. He was not scheduled to take office for another year.

By January 1863, Garfield—healthy again—was ordered back in the field to battle the Confederates. For several months, he served as chief of staff to General William Rosecrans. Garfield's job was to make sure that Rosecrans's orders were carried out by all the officers under the general's command.

Later that year, both joy and tragedy struck the Garfields. In October, James and Lucretia welcomed their second child, Harry. Sadly, just a few weeks later, their three-year-old daughter, Trot, developed diphtheria and died. No antibiotics existed to treat the disease. A vaccine to protect children was sixty years away.

Trot's unexpected death struck Garfield hard. He wrote his wife two weeks afterward, "I still struggle with my grief and think [of] our precious darling with such a yearning agony of heartbreak that at times it seems as though I could not endure it."

This photograph of Lucretia was taken around 1870, when she was thirty-eight.

ON TO THE HOUSE

Garfield intended to remain in the army until the war was over. But without an end in sight, President Lincoln asked him to take his seat in the House of Representatives instead. To put down the Confederate rebellion, the president required votes in Congress from men who would back the needs of the military. Having achieved the rank of major general, Garfield resigned his U.S. Army commission in early December 1863.

He had been a carpenter, janitor, teacher, preacher, college president, lawyer, state senator, and general. Now James Abram Garfield, age thirty-two, was a U.S. congressman. He had made great strides from his log-cabin birth, though his path to this point had not been easy.

"I lament sorely that I was born to poverty," he once told a friend. Yet Garfield was optimistic about his future. "Poverty is very inconvenient," he later wrote, "but it is a fine spur to activity, and may be made a rich blessing."

THE GARFIELD FAMILY

Throughout Garfield's early years in Congress, the family lived in rented rooms in Washington, returning to their house in Hiram, Ohio, during Congressional holidays. After he'd been in office several years, Garfield sold the Ohio house and built one in Washington.

Late in 1876, during his seventh term, Garfield bought a farm in Mentor, Ohio, about twenty miles from where he was born. With the help of hired hands, Garfield grew crops and raised animals to supplement the income from his government position and law practice. It was important to him that his children experience the hard work of farming, and the family spent the summer and school holidays there.

Five of the seven Garfield children survived to adulthood. *Left to right:* Mary (Mollie, b. 1867), James (Jim, b. 1865), Harry (Hal, b. 1863), Irvin (Irv, b. 1870), and Abram (Abe, b. 1872). Garfield enjoyed reading to his children, often from Shakespeare, but he regretted that his career frequently got in the way. "It is a pity that I have so little time to devote to my children," he wrote in his diary in May 1873.

Garfield took great interest in his children. During one ten-year period (1870–1879), he recorded how many inches each child grew per year.

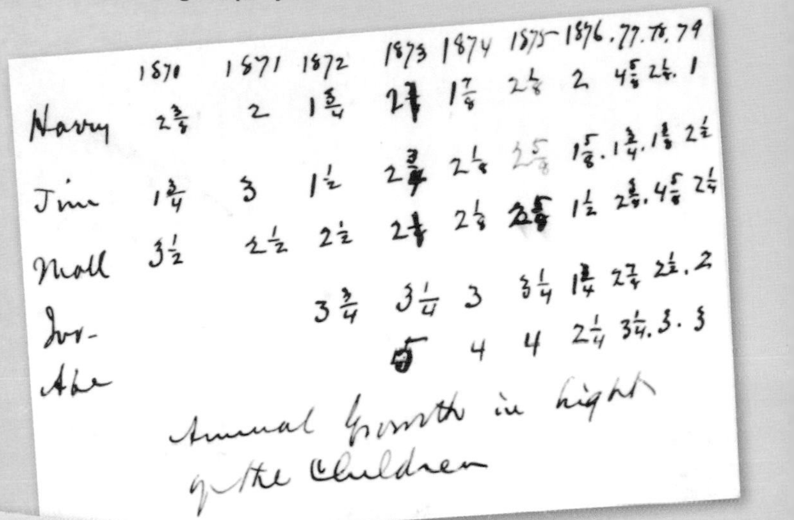

	1870	1871	1872	1873	1874	1875	1876	77	78	79
Harry	2 3/8	2	1 3/4	2 7/8	1 7/8	2 1/8	2	4 5/8	2 1/4	1
Jim	1 3/4	3	1 1/2	2 3/4	2 1/8	2 5/8	1 5/8	1 3/4	1 3/8	2 1/2
Moll	3 1/2	2 1/2	2 1/2	2 7/8	2 1/8	2 5/8	1 1/2	2 3/8	4 5/8	2 1/4
Irv-			3 3/4	3 1/4	3	3 1/4	1 3/4	2 3/4	2 1/2	2
Abe				5	4	4	2 1/4	3 1/4	3	3

Annual Growth in hight of the Children

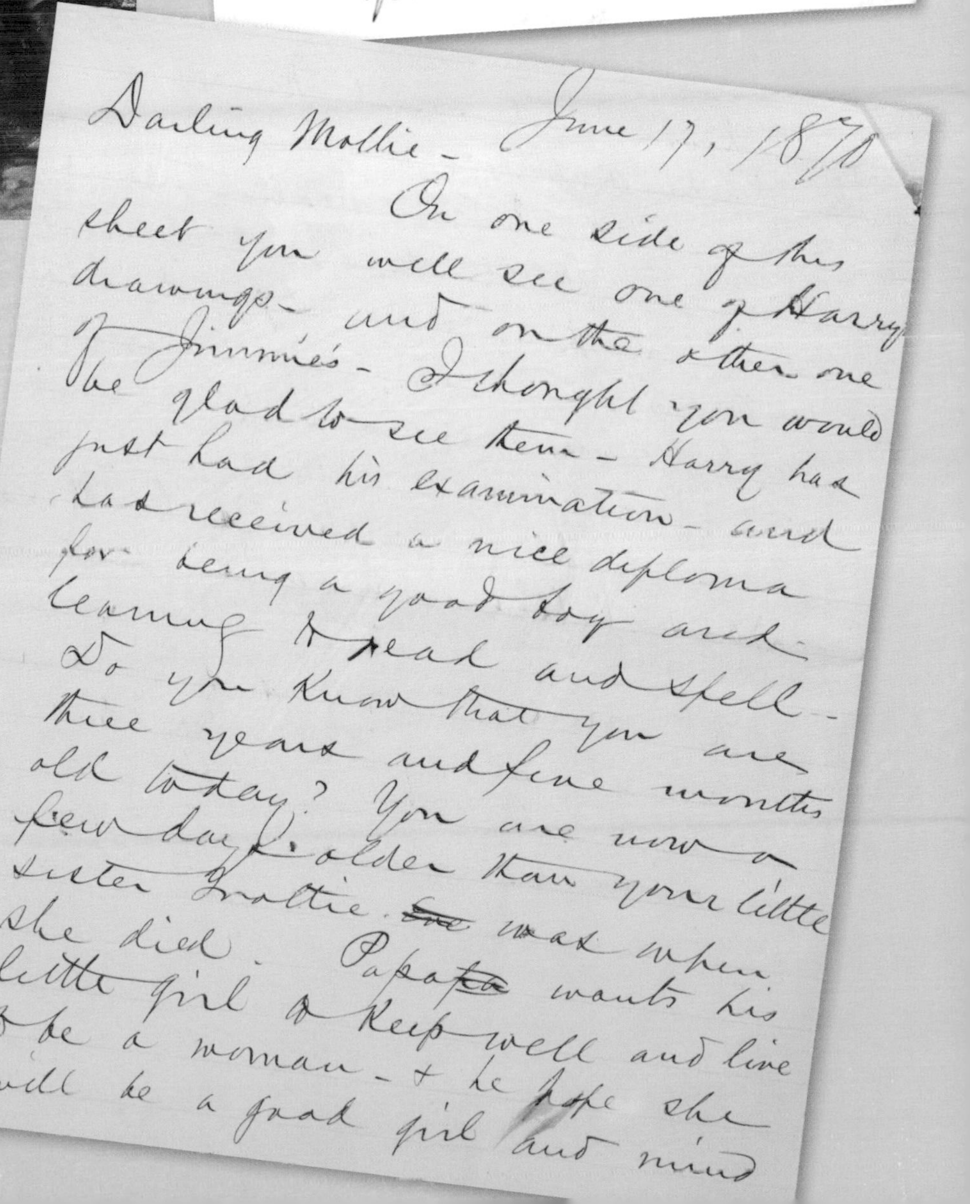

Darling Mollie – June 17, 1870

On one side of this sheet you will see one of Harry's drawings – and on the other one of Jimmie's – I thought you would be glad to see them – Harry has just had his examination – and had received a nice diploma for being a good boy and learning to read and spell – Do you know that you are three years and five months old today? You are now a few days older than your little sister Trottie was when she died. Papa wants his little girl to keep well and live to be a woman – & he hopes she will be a good girl and mind

James Garfield was devastated by the December 1, 1863, loss of his first child, Eliza (Trot), who died at age three. Garfield wrote this letter on June 17, 1870, to his second daughter, Mollie (pictured with her father that year). It reads: "Do you know that you are three years and five months old today? You are now a few days older than your little sister Trottie was when she died. Papa wants his little girl to keep well and live to be a woman." (Mollie lived to be eighty.)

Thirteen years after Trot's death, Garfield buried his son Edward (Neddie), who died of whooping cough a couple of months shy of his second birthday. No vaccine existed to protect children from this killer disease until the 1940s. In his diary on October 27, 1876, two days after Neddie's death, Garfield wrote, "I did not know . . . that my heart could be so wrung again by a similar loss."

CHAPTER THREE
A DARK HORSE

"He had in him those elements of a sturdy manhood
that would lead to sure success."

—*Harper's Weekly*

I N EARLY DECEMBER 1863, GARFIELD TOOK HIS SEAT IN THE HOUSE OF
Representatives. The Republican leadership assigned him to the Military Affairs
Committee. As President Lincoln had hoped, Garfield energetically supported the
armed forces in the Union's efforts to end the Civil War.

Garfield also pushed for passage of the Thirteenth Amendment to abolish slavery, a change
in the Constitution favored by Lincoln and the Republican Party. In a January 1865 speech
in the House, Garfield said, "This body of slavery lies before us among the dead enemies of
the republic, mortally wounded, impotent in its fiendish wickedness." The amendment was
ratified by the states and became part of the Constitution in December 1865.

Garfield rejoiced as the Civil War ended in spring 1865, but Lincoln's assassination shocked
him. Two days after the president's death, he wrote Lucretia from New York, where he was on
business, "My heart is so broken with our great national loss that I can hardly think or
write or speak."

A print shows an artist's version of the assassination of President Abraham Lincoln at Ford's Theatre in Washington on April 14, 1865. *Left to right:* John Wilkes Booth; Lincoln; his wife, Mary Todd Lincoln; and the Lincolns' guests, Major Henry Rathbone and Clara Harris.

THE ASSASSINATION OF
ABRAHAM LINCOLN

On April 14, 1865, President Lincoln and his wife attended a play at Ford's Theatre in Washington. As he sat in the theatre's presidential box facing the stage, Abraham Lincoln had no special protection. The U.S. Secret Service wasn't established until July 1865, and even then, it didn't guard the president. As part of the Department of the Treasury, its purpose was to fight counterfeiting. Congress did not assign presidential safety to the Secret Service until 1901.

About 10:15 that April evening, while Lincoln was enjoying the play, John Wilkes Booth opened the unguarded door to the president's box. Seconds later, he fired his pistol into the back of Lincoln's head. Without regaining consciousness, Abraham Lincoln died the next morning.

Booth and his coconspirators, all of whom sympathized with the Confederacy, planned to assassinate others in a simultaneous attack that evening. At the theatre, Booth had expected to also kill Union general Ulysses Grant. But Grant changed his mind about attending the play with Lincoln. Lewis Powell forced his way into the home of Secretary of State William Seward, slashing him in his bed. Seward survived the attack, and Powell was later captured. The man assigned to kill Vice President Andrew Johnson was too afraid to carry out his mission.

After shooting Lincoln, Booth escaped. Twelve days later, the Union military tracked him down in Virginia, where he was fatally shot. Four of his accomplices were convicted and hanged on July 7, 1865. Four others went to prison.

Along with other congressional Republicans, Garfield came to oppose the actions of Lincoln's successor, Andrew Johnson. He thought that Johnson, a Democrat sympathetic to the South, didn't do enough to protect freed Blacks and stop violence and unrest in the defeated southern states.

With the war over, Garfield moved to the Appropriations Committee, which monitored the government's finances and spending. A skilled debater, he advocated for the interests of farmers and businessmen in his district. His constituents reelected him eight more times.

Garfield continued to practice law, including an 1866 appearance before the U.S. Supreme Court. The case involved Indiana citizens convicted by a military tribunal of conspiring to aid the Confederacy during the war. Garfield argued that the case should have been handled by an Indiana civilian court, not the military. The Supreme Court agreed.

Garfield, age forty-eight, in 1880

Garfield often traveled by train within Ohio and to various states, giving speeches and boosting other Republican candidates. This gained him friends and political allies.

On the train and in his free time, Garfield read. Early in his life, he had limited access to books. Now he could afford to buy them for his home library. A frequent visitor to the Library of Congress, Garfield asked the librarians for book recommendations, which he borrowed or purchased to expand his knowledge of history, philosophy, and other subjects.

SPOILS

In 1868, former Union general Ulysses Grant was elected president, succeeding Andrew Johnson. Although Grant was a fellow Republican, Garfield did not agree with many of his policies and actions. He became alarmed by the way the new president was giving government jobs to unqualified people at the request of party politicians.

Under the patronage (or spoils) system, an election's winning party filled thousands of positions. A person's knowledge, skills, and competence were unimportant. Instead, political bosses awarded these jobs to friends and loyal associates who donated money or helped with the campaign.

Garfield wrote a friend, "The rush for office is absolutely appalling; it would almost seem that the adult population of the United States had moved on the works of the government and were determined to carry every position by storm."

During Grant's eight-year administration, from 1869 to 1877, tensions grew between two factions of the Republican party. The Stalwarts enjoyed substantial influence in filling government jobs. Others wanted to reform the spoils system. Because members of this group criticized Grant, the Stalwarts accused them of being only half-Republican and labeled them Half-Breeds.

James Garfield tried to stay neutral in the disagreements, though he more often aligned with those who promoted reform of government hiring practices.

BATTLE LINES DRAWN

In 1876, an Ohio Republican named Rutherford Hayes became president after a close election that had to be settled in the House of Representatives. Garfield was pleased when President Hayes attempted reforms to the spoils system, but Hayes had little success. The beleaguered president decided not to run for a second term. And in 1880, a battle broke out over who would be the Republican Party's presidential candidate.

In early June 1880, Republican delegates and spectators gathered in the Chicago convention hall to nominate their candidates for president and vice president. This illustration appeared in *Harper's Weekly*, June 19, 1880. The weekly magazine's coverage of events usually lagged by a couple of weeks because of the time needed for publication.

As the nominating convention began in Chicago in early June 1880, politicians took sides. Roscoe Conkling and the Stalwarts supported former President Grant for an unprecedented third term. Under President Hayes, the Stalwarts lost power, and they wanted it back.

Opposing them were the Half-Breeds, who considered Grant a losing candidate because many voters had become disgusted by the scandals and corruption during his time in office. Their candidate was Senator James Blaine.

Besides Grant and Blaine, the other candidate seeking the nomination was John Sherman of Ohio, a former U.S. senator and the current secretary of treasury under President Hayes.

STALWARTS AND HALF-BREEDS

During the 1870s, the Republican Party split into factions. The Stalwarts were led by **Senator Roscoe Conkling** of New York (left), and the Half-Breeds organized behind **Senator James Blaine** of Maine.

Conkling (1829–1888), a lawyer, served in the House of Representatives before joining the Senate in 1867. At six foot three inches tall, he intimidated both enemies and allies with his imposing stature and sharp tongue. James Blaine (1830–1893), a former newspaper editor, was a member of the House of Representatives from 1863 until 1876, rising to Speaker of the House in 1869. He became a senator in 1876.

Fifteen thousand delegates, spectators, and news reporters filled Chicago's huge Interstate Industrial Exposition Building. Delegates were deeply divided by the rift in the party, and the convention floor was raucous and loud.

James Garfield went to the convention as part of the Ohio delegation and gave a speech nominating fellow Ohioan Sherman. In it, he pleaded for party unity.

After a full day of voting for a nominee, the delegates couldn't agree on a candidate. Neither Grant, Blaine, nor Sherman garnered enough votes to earn the nomination. The exhausted delegates adjourned for the day. It looked less and less likely that one of the three men could win, and some delegates began looking for a compromise candidate.

Perhaps James Garfield was the right man to break the convention's deadlock. He was well known for his years in Congress and his dedication to the Republican Party. Garfield was respected for his ability to work with those of different viewpoints, and he had given the delegates a stirring address calling for party harmony.

The next afternoon, on the thirty-fourth ballot, the Wisconsin delegation attempted to end the two-day stalemate. When the clerk asked for Wisconsin's vote, the head of the state's delegation stood up and announced two votes for Grant, two votes for Blaine . . . and sixteen votes for Garfield. On the next ballot, other states shifted to Garfield, giving him a few dozen votes.

On the thirty-sixth ballot, everything changed. Many more delegates switched their votes to Garfield. A reporter described the convention hall where "thousands of men and women present were on their feet yelling 'Garfield, Garfield, Garfield.'" By the end of the roll call, James Abram Garfield had won enough votes to become the Republican Party's nominee, beating out Grant, Blaine, and Sherman.

When Garfield arrived in Chicago, he didn't expect to leave as the presidential candidate. He had become the convention's surprise dark horse.

On the night of June 8, after Garfield received the Republican Party's nomination, he sent this telegram from Chicago to Lucretia in Mentor, informing her of his nomination. It reads: "Dear Wife, If the result meets your approval, I shall be content. love to all the household."

The Republicans knew they needed Grant's backers— Conkling and the Stalwarts— to rally voters and raise money for the campaign. A group of party leaders offered the vice-presidential nomination to Chester Arthur of New York. Arthur had never run for public office, but he was one of Conkling's closest friends.

THE DEMOCRATS' EDGE

At their convention later in June, the Democrats nominated Winfield Scott Hancock as their candidate. Hancock was a career soldier, a U.S. Army general in the Civil War, and a hero at the Battle of Gettysburg. Although Hancock had never held elected office, he had an edge in the election.

He was based in New York, and his running mate, William English, had been a congressman from Indiana. The winning ticket in these two states would collect a large number of votes in the Electoral College. And importantly, Hancock could count on winning all the southern states where the Democratic Party now dominated.

Chester Arthur (1829–1886) was born in Vermont. Like Garfield, he taught in a country school before studying to become a lawyer. During President Grant's administration, Arthur served as Collector of Customs at the Port in New York, a political appointment arranged by Roscoe Conkling. The position allowed Conkling and Arthur to hand out hundreds of well-paying jobs to friends and supporters. President Hayes, who attempted to reform the spoils system during his administration, defied Conkling by replacing Arthur. At the time of the 1880 convention, Arthur was practicing law. Just six months earlier, his wife had died suddenly of pneumonia, leaving him with two school-aged children to raise.

Since the war, the party's power in the South had gradually increased. Democrats were popular among White southerners because the party had pushed for leniency toward the Confederacy and had supported efforts to deny former slaves the vote.

For several years after the war's end, federal soldiers were stationed in the former Confederate states. They helped to guarantee the voting rights granted to Black males by the Fifteenth Amendment of 1870. Most former slaves voted for the Republicans, Lincoln's party, with some Black men winning election to political office.

But by 1880, the troops had been pulled out. Without that protection, Blacks all over the South were prevented from voting by intimidation and violence at the hands of White southerners. As the campaign of 1880 began, the Democratic Party controlled the majority of votes in the South.

THE CAMPAIGN

Before 1880, presidential candidates did not directly campaign for themselves. Instead, their supporters promoted them by delivering speeches around the country. Garfield, one of the Republicans' most accomplished orators, modified this tradition. He stayed at his farm in Mentor, Ohio, and encouraged the public to come there to hear him speak.

People came in droves. Many took the train that stopped at the back end of Garfield's property. Others reached his farm by horse and carriage along the road out front. Garfield stood on his porch and spoke about his views and plans for governing. The national press regularly reported on his campaign speeches, calling his farm *Lawnfield*. Garfield adopted the name.

During the almost five months between his nomination and the election, Garfield gave dozens of speeches to his visitors. A delegation of nine hundred women from Cleveland. Iron and steel workers. Civil War veterans. College students. A group of one thousand businessmen.

In late September, the Jubilee Singers arrived from Fisk University in Nashville, Tennessee, a school established in 1866 for Black students. Garfield invited them into his parlor, where they sang several spirituals for his family and neighbors. Afterward, Garfield commented on the importance of the students' education in helping them reach their goals. It was a lesson his own life had taught him. Voicing his support for his guests and for other Black citizens, he added, "I would rather be with you and defeated than against you and victorious."

ARRIVAL OF VIS

An illustration from *Frank Leslie's Illustrated Newspaper*, December 18, 1880, shows visitors arriving at Garfield's front porch.

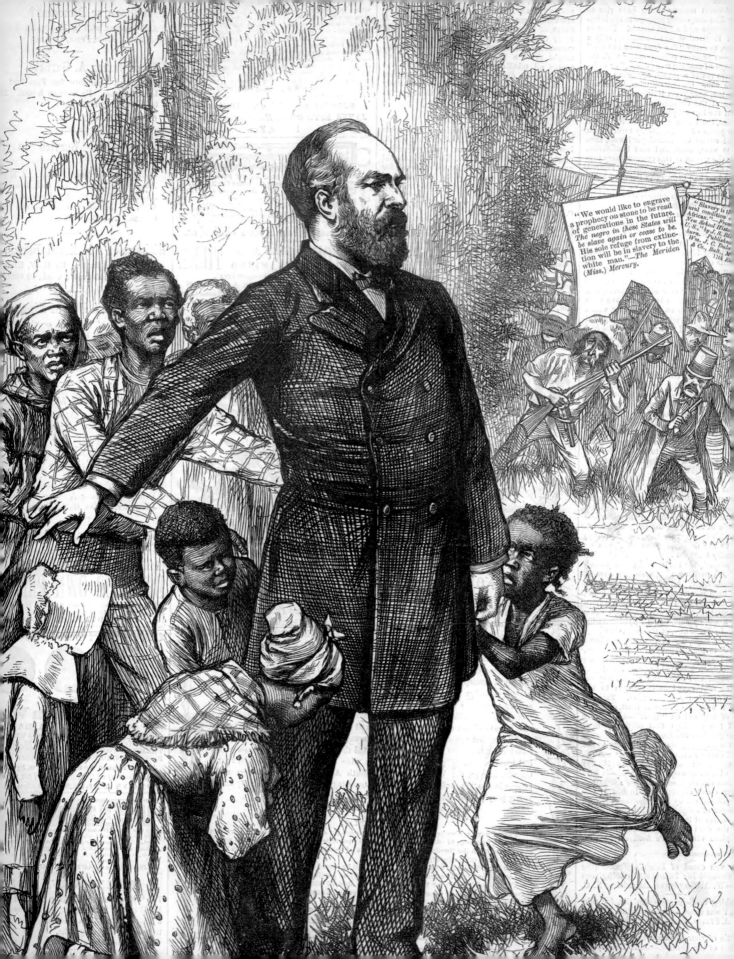

"We would like to engrave a prophecy on stone to be read of generations in the future. The negro in these States will be slave again or cease to be. His sole refuge from extinction will be in slavery to the white man."—*The Meriden (Miss.) Mercury.*

The house at Lawnfield as it looks today. Garfield gave campaign speeches from this porch. He had an expressive baritone voice and knew how to hold a crowd's attention.

By Election Day, more than fifteen thousand people had shown up at Lawnfield. Unfortunately, besides trampling the grass, some of them vandalized Garfield's farm. As mementos, visitors stole ears of corn from the field and sawed young fruit trees into pieces of wood. One even cut a horse blanket into souvenir pieces.

Garfield established a campaign office in a small building behind the house that he used for his library. The office had a telegraph connection to keep him informed of progress by Republican campaigners throughout the country. He hired Joseph Stanley Brown, age twenty-two, as his secretary. Brown helped with letters and telegram correspondence.

In his campaign, Garfield reminded voters of the Democratic Party's connections to slavery and the rebellious South. He pointed out that Republicans had given citizenship to four million slaves. His party restored the country to economic strength after the costly southern rebellion. Garfield promised prosperity for working people and a peaceful nation in which they could raise and educate their children.

Garfield's supporters emphasized his rise from poverty, presenting him as a common man who could relate to the everyday lives of voters. His backers published numerous biographies to tell his story: *From the Log Cabin to the White*

Joseph Stanley Brown (at the desk), James Garfield, and a visitor in the campaign office behind the candidate's house in Mentor, Ohio. This illustration appeared in *Frank Leslie's Illustrated Newspaper*, December 18, 1880.

GENL. GARFIELDS BUSINESS OFFICE

House, From Canal Boy to President, and *From the Tow Path to the White House.*

Grant, Blaine, and Sherman, despite losing the Republican nomination, campaigned for Garfield. So did Conkling.

A DECISION MADE

Election Day, November 2, 1880, was sunny in Ohio. Garfield spent a quiet day writing letters and working around his farm. After he voted in town, he returned home in the afternoon to await the election results.

That evening, the news from each state gradually came in by telegraph to Lawnfield's campaign office. The popular vote was extremely close. But by 3:00 a.m., Garfield was confident that he had taken the majority in enough states to win decisively in the Electoral College.

He had never lost an election, and he didn't lose this one—the most

A campaign poster for the Garfield-Arthur team. It included detailed biographies of both men as well as the Republican Party's platform.

important of his life. He had managed to hold together the Republicans' factions and keep the White House under the party's control.

Garfield was too busy to savor his victory. Well-wishers to the farm had to be welcomed. Letters to his supporters had to be written. A cabinet had to be chosen. Plans had to be made for assuming the presidency in four months, on March 4, 1881.

James Garfield had served in government long enough to anticipate "a life of <u>increasing</u> <u>care</u> and <u>anxiety</u>." In his final diary entry before turning the page to 1881, he wrote, "I close the year with a sad conviction that I am bidding good-by to the freedom of private life, and to a long series of happy years, which I fear terminate with 1880."

THE ELECTION.

The Country Safe for Another Four Years.

GARFIELD ELECTED PRESIDENT.

An Almost Solid North Overwhelms the Solid South.

IMMENSE REPUBLICAN GAINS.

Elation Upon One Side, Depression Upon the Other.

[SPECIAL BY TELEGRAPH TO THE RECORD-UNION.]

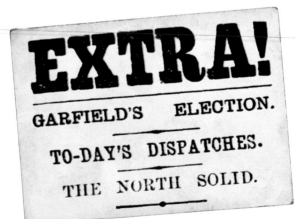

EXTRA!

GARFIELD'S ELECTION.

TO-DAY'S DISPATCHES.

THE NORTH SOLID.

On Wednesday, November 3, 1880, headlines across the country announced Garfield's victory. These are from the *Evening Star* of Washington, DC (left), and the *Sacramento* [CA] *Daily Record-Union* (top).

CHAPTER FOUR
THE LONER

"I thought he was a fool or crazy and had no patience with him."

—John Guiteau, brother of Charles Guiteau

T HE DAY AFTER THE NOVEMBER
election, Charles Julius Guiteau was
ecstatic when he read about the
Republican victory in the newspapers. Now
James Garfield would reward him for his hard
work in the campaign: The advice Guiteau provided.
The speeches he gave. The time he volunteered
at headquarters. *His* efforts put Garfield and
Arthur in power, and that meant that Guiteau
soon would have an important position in the
new administration.

Or so he thought.

An illustration from *Harper's Weekly*, November 20, 1880, depicts
Garfield as a victorious Roman chariot racer. Arthur rides a horse
next to the chariot.

VOL. XI.

FIRST EDITION.
11:30 P. M.

CONFIRMED

SUCH IS THE STATE OF THE
GLORIOUS NEWS OF
YESTERDAY.

The Victory Complete and Overwhelming Everywhere.

A Solid North with Possibly one
State Excepted.

Both Houses of Congress and the
Entire Government

Redeemed from the Menace of a
Solid South.

Let Songs of Praise Ascend to
Heaven for the Results.

Knoxville *Daily* **Chronicle.**

NO. 135

KNOXVILLE, TENN.: THURSDAY MORNING, NOVEMBER 4, 1880.

GARFIELD & ARTHUR

The front page of a Tennessee newspaper announces the Garfield-Arthur victory, calling it "glorious news." Charles Guiteau believed that he had played an important part in electing Garfield.

SOMETHING WRONG

Charles Guiteau was a loner, but not because he wanted to be. People often told him to go away. Others avoided him. It had been the story of his life.

Charles was born ten years after James Garfield in the northern Illinois town of Freeport on September 8, 1841. He was only seven when his sickly mother died. His father, who worked as a store merchant, court clerk, and bank cashier, remarried five years after his wife's death.

In Charles's mind, neither his father nor stepmother showed him much affection. He claimed his father was harsh and beat him when he fidgeted or mispronounced words. John Guiteau, who was seven years older than Charles, found his brother to be difficult and wanted nothing to do with him. Charles felt that only his older sister, Frances, was kind.

Charles left home at sixteen, but he couldn't hold a job or support himself. Frances and her husband took him in for a while, until his maternal grandfather died and bequeathed Charles enough money to pay for college. Although he was keen to go to university, he wasn't able to pass the entrance exams.

Floundering and directionless, Charles turned to religion. In 1860, when he was not yet nineteen, his devout father urged him to join a religious commune in Oneida, New York, run by a man his father admired. Charles used his inheritance to become a member.

At first, he was enthusiastic. He refused, however, to do the menial jobs required of members to sustain the community. Charles considered himself too talented and intelligent for kitchen and factory work.

Others in the Oneida commune regarded him as moody, swinging from spirited to sullen within minutes. Charles imagined that he was charming and handsome. But the women ridiculed him, calling him "Gitout." He hated the community's practice of offering criticisms of members' behavior in order to encourage self-improvement. The group charged that Charles was conceited and vain, having an opinion of himself that exceeded reality. He knew that was a lie.

The Mansion House at the Oneida Community in Oneida, New York, around the time when Charles Guiteau was one of more than two hundred members living there. The religious group believed that, through prayer and spiritual education, a person had the potential to become free of sin and perfect in all things. The group also believed that this was best done in an isolated community in which everyone shared the same beliefs.

His family suspected something was wrong with him. So did the Oneida leaders. One of them wrote Charles's father to say that they believed there was "much evidence of an unsound insane mind."

BIG DREAMS

Guiteau spent the Civil War years at the commune. After about five years as a member, he came up with the idea of going to New York City and launching a religious newspaper. The Oneida leadership encouraged him to leave.

His plan to be a journalist failed miserably. No one would invest, advertise, or subscribe to his newspaper. Out of money, Charles borrowed from his father and his sister and futilely tried to sue the Oneida Community for money he said they owed him.

GUITEAU IN JULY 1869.

Charles Julius Guiteau (1841–1882), around age twenty-eight, in an illustration from a book published in 1882

Next, convinced that he could become a well-known attorney, Guiteau found an apprentice position in a Chicago law firm. It was easy to get an Illinois law license in 1868, and after several months, Guiteau learned enough to pass the simple oral examination. Having a law license didn't get him much business, however. He was incompetent and incoherent when arguing a case in court.

While living in Chicago, Guiteau persuaded a young woman named Annie Bunn that he was a prosperous attorney and churchgoing Baptist. She married him after a short courtship but soon realized that her husband was obsessed with wealth and fame. Annie watched Guiteau prance back and forth in front of a mirror. "Don't you think I would look like a good Foreign Minister?" he asked her. She knew better than to tell him the truth.

Guiteau had an uncontrollable temper that was set off when anyone disagreed with or offended him. He physically abused Annie, locked her in a closet, cheated on her with other women, and forced her to borrow money and lie to landlords to whom he owed rent.

A skillful con artist, Guiteau routinely manipulated people into helping

WIFE OF GUITEAU, IN 1869.

A sketch of Annie Bunn Guiteau in 1869, early in her marriage to Charles Guiteau

him. He gained trust by acting pleasant and friendly. Then he talked the person into lending him cash. Even though Guiteau didn't pay back the first loan, he often tricked a sympathetic lender into giving him more.

Guiteau always had an excuse to explain why he couldn't repay a debt and needed to borrow again. His wife later said, "I presume no one ever had any dealings with him where money was involved, that did not get the worst of the transaction."

Business associates, friends, and family eventually abandoned Guiteau when they discovered he had swindled them. On a few occasions, his scams got him arrested and jailed for a short period.

Finally, like everyone else Guiteau deceived, his wife had enough. "It was impossible to believe anything he said," she recalled, "unless one knew it to be a fact from other information." In 1874, after less than five years of marriage, she divorced him on grounds of adultery.

CAMPAIGN WORKER

Having failed as a journalist and lawyer, Guiteau moved on to new schemes. In 1876, he began writing a book about religion called *The Truth*. It was heavily plagiarized from a work written thirty years earlier by the Oneida Community's founder.

A cartoon from *Harper's Weekly*, July 31, 1880, highlights why some voters preferred James Garfield, an experienced U.S. congressman, over Democratic candidate General Winfield Scott Hancock (depicted in his uniform), who had never been elected to a government office. The caption reads: "Uncle Sam: 'But you don't seem to have any other recommendations, and we would rather let it to a Statesman.'"

Guiteau set off on a tour throughout the Midwest and East to make money lecturing about his views on the Second Coming of Christ. Local newspapers panned his lecture as rambling nonsense, and he couldn't attract audiences. Guiteau blamed others and gave elaborate explanations for his failure.

When James Garfield and Chester Arthur ran for office in 1880, Guiteau saw an opportunity to reach his ambition of becoming a great and famous man. Someday, he was sure, he "should be President of the United States." The campaign would help him move closer to achieving that goal.

After the Republican nominating convention in June, Guiteau left Boston, where he had been unsuccessfully selling life insurance, and traveled to New York City. His plan was to show Republican leaders that he was a valuable asset to the campaign. In return, Guiteau expected to be rewarded with a political job when Garfield won

The cover of *Harper's Weekly* on November 20, 1880, celebrates the Republican Party's victory over its Democratic opponents. The artist was Thomas Nast (1840–1902), who was the first to use an elephant as the Republican symbol. Nast singles out New Jersey because it was the one northern state that did not go for Garfield.

HARPER'S WEEKLY.

JOURNAL OF CIVILIZATION.

VOL. XXIV.—No. 1247.]   NEW YORK, SATURDAY, NOVEMBER 20, 1880.   [SINGLE COPIES TEN CENTS.
$4.00 PER YEAR IN ADVANCE.

Entered according to Act of Congress, in the Year 1880, by Harper & Brothers, in the Office of the Librarian of Congress, at Washington.

THE REPUBLICAN PACHYDERM ALIVE AND KICKING.

the election. He spent his days hanging around the Republican Party headquarters on Fifth Avenue.

In early August, Guiteau took along a campaign speech he'd written, "Garfield Against Hancock." He handed it out to politicians at the headquarters, including Chester Arthur and Roscoe Conkling, hoping they'd let him deliver it to an audience. "They seemed to be highly pleased with it," Guiteau told himself.

The campaign wasn't as impressed as Guiteau thought. No one was much interested in using him or his speech. He concluded it was because they didn't think he could draw a big enough crowd. "I had ideas, but I did not have a national reputation," he said. Finally, the Republican Party relented and allowed Guiteau to give his speech, only once, to a group of Black voters in New York City.

Although Guiteau visited campaign headquarters frequently, his role in the election of Garfield and Arthur was limited to that single speech. Still, Guiteau considered himself friendly with Chester Arthur and a key to Garfield's election. He was confident the new president would give him a valuable role in his administration, preferably a diplomatic appointment.

Early in March 1881, Charles Guiteau departed New York, leaving unpaid bills behind as he usually did, and headed to Washington to claim his new job.

In four months, he would have the fame he had long sought.

On November 11, 1880, nine days after Garfield's victory, Guiteau wrote this letter to William Evarts, the current secretary of state under President Hayes. In it, Guiteau asks for confirmation that the president-elect would fill all diplomatic positions with new men. Guiteau was certain that he would have a better chance of receiving a political job from Garfield because he had campaigned for him.

N.y., Nov. 11 '80.

Hon. Wm. M. Evarts
   Dear Sir:
            I wish to ask you a question? If President Garfield appoints Mr. A. to a foreign mission does that superceed President Hayes commission for the same appointment? Do not all foreign ministers appointed by President Hayes retire on March 4 next? Please answer me, at the 5th. Ave Hotel, at your earliest convenience. I am solid for Gen. Garfield & may get an important appointment from him next spring.

               Yours very truly
                  Charles Guiteau

Inauguration of James Garfield at the U.S. Capitol building, March 4, 1881. (Beginning in 1937, Inauguration Day has been held on its current date of January 20.) After taking the oath of office, Garfield bent down to kiss his mother. Eliza Garfield, age seventy-nine, was the first woman to be present at her son's presidential inauguration. Afterward, she lived in the White House. In mid-May, she traveled to Ohio to spend the summer with her two daughters and their families, away from the muggy Washington weather.

CHAPTER FIVE
THE VOW

"I must confront the problem of trying to survive the Presidency."

—President-Elect James Garfield

ON MARCH 3, 1881, THE NIGHT BEFORE HIS INAUGURATION, James Garfield stayed up late writing his speech.

It wasn't that he didn't know what he wanted to say to the nation. And it wasn't that he had trouble putting words together. Garfield was an expert at doing that. He was used to thinking on his feet during debates, coming up with just the right words on the spur of the moment.

But his inauguration speech had to be special, and Garfield wasn't satisfied with his first draft. Two days before, he decided to rewrite the speech. Now, with only several hours left until he took the oath of office, he still hadn't had enough time to finish.

MAKING PEACE

Long before Garfield and his family boarded the train from Mentor to Washington a few days earlier, he had toiled over naming his cabinet members. To have an effective and strong administration, he needed to bring together the Republican Party's warring factions. He faced a difficult challenge in representing all regions of the country; satisfying Conkling and the Stalwarts; reaching out to James Blaine and the Half-Breeds; and soothing the bad feelings of allies like John Sherman, from whom he'd taken the nomination.

The secretary of state, in charge of foreign affairs, was considered the most influential cabinet member, more essential than the vice president. For this post, Garfield chose Blaine. The two men entered the House of Representatives at the same time and had worked closely together. Garfield felt comfortable with him.

But even after months of managing egos and matching names and positions, Garfield didn't have the rest of his cabinet in place when he reached Washington.

Since his arrival, his time had been filled with meetings. Many visitors stopped by his hotel to congratulate him. On Inauguration Eve, he'd been invited to dinner with outgoing President Hayes. From there, Garfield joined a group of his Williams College classmates who came to the city to see him take the oath.

He told his old friends of his anxiety: "To-night I am a private citizen. To-morrow I shall be called to assume new responsibilities, and on the day after the broadside of the world's wrath will strike. It will strike hard."

After retiring to his hotel that evening, Garfield finally had the chance to polish his inaugural speech. He didn't get to bed until after 2:30 a.m.

THE NEW PRESIDENT

On Friday morning, March 4, 1881, after sleeping only a few hours, Garfield awoke to sleet and snow. By midday, when he took his place in front of the Capitol building, the sun had come out and the streets were slushy. Fifty thousand people stood before him, waiting to hear his voice.

In his thirty-five-minute speech, Garfield addressed the crowd—and the

The new president (on his feet in the center front row) and his family watch the inauguration parade from the elaborate reviewing stand. More than fifteen thousand marchers participated, including bands, soldiers, and groups of Civil War veterans.

millions of Americans who would later read his words in their hometown newspapers. He referred to the Civil War sixteen years earlier and the lingering tensions between North and South. Future generations will be grateful, he said, "that the Union was preserved, that slavery was overthrown, and that both races were made equal before the law." He vowed to protect the voting rights of Blacks in the South.

As a former educator, Garfield decried the nation's high rate of illiteracy, particularly in the South, revealed by questions in the 1880 census asking if a person could read and write. In the entire U.S., 17 percent of those older than age ten were unable to write. Among "colored persons" in that age group, the rate was 70 percent. The success of democracy depended on educated voters, he said. If the next generation "comes to its inheritance blinded by ignorance . . . , the fall of the Republic will be certain and remediless."

Garfield pledged to use his congressional experience with the country's finances to keep the economy strong and to prevent wasteful government spending. Recognizing the public's disdain for the spoils system, he called for a law regulating civil service jobs within the government.

By the end of his speech, Garfield was hoarse. He had strained to make his voice loud enough to be heard by the large crowd.

The chief justice of the Supreme Court stepped forward to administer the oath of office. And James Abram Garfield became the twentieth president of the United States, a sprawling country of 50 million people.

The following day Garfield began his presidency, getting a bitter taste of what lay ahead. "The crowd of callers commence[d] early and continued in great force," he recorded in his diary that night.

Garfield had been a congressman for seventeen years. He knew how government worked, how vicious politics was, and how people with special interests tried to influence and manipulate lawmakers with words or favors. Yet he wasn't prepared for what greeted him as soon as he won the election.

Thanks to the political patronage system, still in place despite President Hayes's efforts to fix it, Garfield was expected to fill thousands of government positions.

The parade of job seekers had started even before he took office. A month after the election, he wrote in his diary, "Almost every one who comes to me wants something which he thinks I can and ought to give him."

The onslaught was worse once he moved into the White House. After one exasperating day, Garfield said to his personal secretary, Joseph Stanley Brown, "These people are merciless; they demand blood, flesh, and brains."

Joseph Stanley Brown (1858–1941) was only twenty-two when he assumed the role of personal secretary to the president. Brown acted as a gatekeeper, limiting who was admitted to Garfield's White House office.

THE JOB SEEKER

Shortly after the inauguration, Charles Guiteau showed up at the White House. He managed to get into the president's office, where Garfield was in conversation with several men.

Guiteau approached the president, handing him a copy of the "Garfield Against Hancock" speech of which he was so proud. Across the top, Guiteau had written "Paris Consulship" with a line drawn to his name. Garfield politely took the speech. Guiteau left, confident that once the president read it, he would respond favorably to Guiteau's request for a diplomatic appointment.

When he didn't hear anything after a few days, Guiteau returned to the White House. This time he was led into a reception room where dozens of other men and women were waiting to see the president.

Guiteau gave his calling card to an usher, whose job it was to greet visitors and escort them to Garfield. The usher sent the card in to Brown along with the cards of everyone else in the reception room. Guiteau was told to take a seat and wait.

A couple of hours passed without his name being called. Undeterred,

Guiteau wrote a brief note and asked the usher to pass it to the president. He sat down and waited some more. After fifteen or twenty minutes, the usher returned. "Mr. Guiteau, the President says it will be impossible for him to see you to-day."

Guiteau left, but he came back less than a week later, presenting his card to the usher as he had done before. Again, his name was not called. Guiteau returned again and again to see Garfield.

Brown noticed Guiteau's frequent visits and knew that the man's request for a diplomatic appointment was the State Department's concern. Certainly, President Garfield didn't have time to meet with him. Brown advised Guiteau to apply to the secretary of state.

But Guiteau "kept coming repeatedly" for weeks, until he was a regular fixture at the White House. Brown politely informed him again that this wasn't a matter the president would handle. Despite Guiteau's personal notes to Garfield, the usher never called his name or gave him a reply from the president. Finally, the White House ushers were instructed that if Guiteau appeared, "he should be quietly kept away."

When Guiteau wasn't trying to see President Garfield, he was busy lobbying at the State Department. He visited Secretary of State James Blaine's office several times over six weeks, and he wrote the secretary numerous letters.

In one, he said, "I think I have a right to claim your help on the strength of this speech." Enclosed was a copy of his "Garfield Against Hancock." Guiteau was sure that it was just a matter of time before he received his reward. "I had every reason to expect that they intended, as soon as they got to it, to give it to me."

Although Blaine was used to persistent office seekers, he became annoyed by this man who was wasting both his and the State Department's time. How could Guiteau possibly imagine he was qualified to be consul-general in Paris? As the United States representative to the French capital, the consul-general was an important position only given to men well known "for intelligence and public service."

Finally, in mid-May, Blaine told Guiteau to his face to stop asking for the position because he had "no prospect whatever of receiving it, and that I did not wish him to mention it to me again."

This did not sit well with Charles Guiteau.

MAKING ONE ENEMY . . .

To James Garfield, dealing with the endless stream of office seekers and politicians was exhausting and monotonous. Some days he had headaches that, he said, "gave me a feeling as if I had been struck a light blow with a hammer." Garfield tried to relax by spending free time with his wife and children. In the evening, he played billiards and read before bed.

Although Garfield filled many government jobs from lists provided by Republican political bosses, he didn't please everyone. In particular, Senator Roscoe Conkling of New York was unhappy. Having his close friend Chester Arthur as vice president wasn't enough for Conkling. He was furious when Garfield refused to name Conkling's choice to the Collector of Customs at the Port of New York.

The majority of imported goods were brought into the country through New York City's port. The Customs House collected tens of millions of dollars in duties on these products, and this money made up a large part of the U.S. government's income.

The jobs at the Customs House were all politically appointed, and Conkling had used the Collector position to win loyalty and power. He expected to have strong influence over Garfield in return for helping to get him elected. Garfield wanted to reduce the corruption surrounding the Customs House, and he didn't like Conkling pushing him around.

A political cartoonist's depiction of James Garfield, January 1881

In retaliation, Conkling tried to stop Garfield's many other nominations from getting necessary Senate approval. His attempts failed, however, and senators supported Garfield.

After this astonishing political loss, Conkling and fellow New York senator and Stalwart ally Thomas Pratt dramatically resigned their Senate seats in mid-May. Because each state legislature chose its U.S. senators (the public didn't vote on Senate candidates), Conkling figured that New York's lawmakers would vote to return them to Washington. This move would strengthen his role as a political leader in New York and in the Senate, while weakening Garfield's power.

But Conkling made a serious miscalculation. The legislature back home decided not to reappoint the two men. Conkling and Pratt lost their Senate seats and influence.

Garfield's decision to oppose Conkling gained him public support. Many people were tired of the spoils system that rewarded corrupt politicians. Garfield felt relieved about the way the battle turned out. "The war of

A political cartoon from *Puck*, April 6, 1881, shows President Garfield on the track to independence from the Stalwarts. The illustrator has drawn the Stalwart bull's head to resemble Roscoe Conkling.

Conkling vs. the administration has passed the first state successfully for me," he wrote in his diary. "It was not of my seeking, but I think he sees by this time that he has undertaken too difficult a task."

. . . AND ADDING ANOTHER

When Charles Guiteau read in the newspapers that Roscoe Conkling had resigned, he was "greatly perplexed and worried." Guiteau had made friends with the Stalwarts while working in New York during the campaign. He considered himself a Stalwart, and he knew they liked him.

James Blaine, who had just rebuffed him, was a long-time Stalwart opponent. With Garfield and the Stalwarts battling and with Conkling resigning, Guiteau feared that his deserved diplomatic appointment was in peril.

He wrote another note to President Garfield. "I have been trying to be your friend; I don't know whether you appreciate it or not . . . Mr. Blaine is a wicked man, and you ought to demand his *immediate* resignation; otherwise you and the Republican party will come to grief. I will see you in the morning, if I can, and talk with you."

Guiteau was not invited to see the president the next day.

Upset by events, Guiteau saw clearly that the factions of the Republican Party must be united. If they weren't, the Democrats or the rebel southerners would take over the country, dooming it to another war.

The terrible situation gnawed at him. One night as he was falling asleep, "an impression came over my mind, like a flash," he later explained, "that if the President was out of the way this whole thing would be solved and everything would go well."

The more he thought about it, the more "it kept growing upon me, pressing me, goading me." Guiteau was convinced it was his responsibility to solve the political crisis, and God was telling him what he had to do. James Abram Garfield had "wrecked the once grand old Republican party, and for this he dies."

As Garfield aged, he gained weight, lost hair, and grew a gray beard.

CHAPTER SIX
STALKING

"My God! what is there in this place
that a man should ever want to get into it?"
—President James Garfield

JAMES GARFIELD'S TROUBLES WITH ROSCOE CONKLING WERE ENDING, thanks to Conkling's own political errors. Yet the job of being president didn't get easier. Garfield's headaches and insomnia continued.

As much as he wanted to tackle the country's problems, he found himself coping daily with bickering in his cabinet, skirmishes with Congress, and endless political appointments. Garfield shared his frustrations with Secretary of State James Blaine. "I have been dealing all these years with ideas," he said, "and here I am dealing only with persons."

CHILLS AND FEVER

The blooming trees and flowers of spring lifted Garfield's spirits, and he enjoyed taking his horse on rides by the Potomac River. But May's warm temperatures triggered a new crisis. Lucretia developed malaria.

Washington was all too familiar with the disease. Stagnant water and swampy spots provided the ideal breeding ground for mosquitoes, which spread malaria among the capital's residents during mild weather. The medical community believed the illness was caused by foul air, called miasma, rising from wet areas. No one realized that the bite of an infected mosquito had sickened the first lady.

Dr. Susan Edson, Lucretia's physician, came to nurse her. At first, Garfield didn't grasp how serious his wife's condition was. But when her chills and high fever became severe and she suffered painful headaches, he feared for her life.

He sat up with her at night. During the day, he was consumed by concern, and he limited the time he spent on presidential business. "My anxiety for her dominates all my thoughts," Garfield wrote in his diary, "and makes me feel that I am fit for nothing."

A cartoon in *Harper's Weekly*, November 26, 1881, sarcastically notes that malaria had become so common in Washington—even among the influential and well-to-do—that it "is a fashionable disease." The drawing by Thomas Nast shows a gentleman shivering with malaria's chills, which typically alternated with high fever. Lucretia Garfield experienced the same symptoms in May and June 1881.

THE POMPS AND VANITIES OF OUR NATIONAL CAPITAL.

Baths of ice water and alcohol lowered Lucretia's temperature, but only temporarily. She was moved to a room on the side of the White House away from the unhealthy river air. Garfield asked his trusted cousin, Dr. Silas Boynton, to travel from Ohio to oversee Lucretia's case.

Over the next month, her fever rose and subsided several times. She slowly regained her appetite and strength, and at last Garfield began to relax. "The dear one is daily improving . . . ," he wrote in his diary on Thursday, June 9, "and every other sorrow fades in the light of the joy her recovery brings."

LURKING DANGER

The day before, Charles Guiteau had taken the first step in his plan. He visited a man he'd met in Michigan many years before, an electrician who had since moved to Washington. Guiteau asked to borrow $15 to cover his boardinghouse bill. He promised to repay the man in a few days when he received $500 due him. One thing Guiteau excelled at was talking people out of their money.

He had run low on cash since arriving in Washington in March. His clothing was worn out, with fraying sleeves and collar. He looked thin and haggard. Guiteau had been able to keep a roof over his head by skipping out on several boardinghouses without paying.

That wasn't why he wanted the money, though. He no longer had a reason to visit the White House and State Department. Instead of seeking a diplomatic appointment, Guiteau had a new, more important mission—one dictated by God. To carry it out, he needed a gun.

Later that Wednesday, Guiteau took the borrowed money to a Washington gun shop a block from the White House. During an earlier visit, he decided on the best weapon—an ivory-handled British revolver. A plainer gun was cheaper, but Guiteau chose a fancy one because, undoubtedly, it would soon be displayed to the world in a museum.

The pistol, a box of ammunition, and a pearl-handled penknife cost him $10. Since Guiteau had never used a gun before, he asked someone at the store to show him how to load it.

Guiteau was determined to make his shots hit their mark when the time came. Twice he went down to the banks of the Potomac River, where no one noticed or cared what he was doing, and practiced firing his new weapon at saplings.

Charles Guiteau, age thirty-nine, around the time he went to Washington in 1881

He knew he couldn't shoot Garfield at the White House, where people were around to stop him. He would have to catch the president outside the building.

Even though Abraham Lincoln had been shot in a theatre sixteen years before, no bodyguards or law enforcement officers accompanied Garfield when he left the White House. Many Americans assumed that presidents in a democracy weren't at risk of assassination. Unlike European monarchs and dictators, an unpopular U.S. leader could be removed by the voters at the ballot box, making assassination unnecessary. In the public's view, Lincoln's killing had been a rare event, perpetrated by Confederates enraged about the South's defeat in the Civil War and fearful of Lincoln's actions in the aftermath.

Resolved to fulfill his mission, Charles Guiteau carefully stalked his victim. He found a spot in Lafayette Park where he could watch the entrance to the White House. He hoped for an opportunity when Garfield left the grounds on horseback, in his carriage, or by foot. Guiteau also monitored reports of the president's schedule in the newspapers, keeping close track of Garfield's movements.

AT THE CHURCH

On Sunday, June 12, four days after Guiteau bought his gun, James Garfield attended Washington's Disciples of Christ Church with his cousin Silas Boynton and Boynton's wife. Although Lucretia felt much better since malaria had sickened her about six weeks earlier, she was still too weak to join them.

Sitting in the wooden pew during the service, Garfield couldn't help thinking that he was being subjected to "a very stupid sermon." He was oblivious to the danger in the church.

Charles Guiteau was close by, intently observing the president from the back of the room. His new pistol was in his pocket. Guiteau liked the idea of removing Garfield while he prayed.

Guiteau waited until the service ended and Garfield exited the church. But he didn't act. After the president drove off in his carriage, Guiteau walked around the side of the building to an open window near Garfield's pew. Gazing inside, he gauged the best aim so that he would hit the back of the president's head without injuring anyone else. He vowed that he "would certainly shoot him" the next time Garfield came to worship.

A few days later, with his mission burning inside him, Guiteau sat down in his rented room and wrote out a letter to the American people. It was essential that everyone understood why he had to murder the president.

James Garfield, he wrote, "proved a traitor to the men that made him, and thereby imperiled the life of the Republic." He wouldn't have won without the help of the Stalwarts, including Guiteau's allies Conkling and Vice President Arthur. Yet Garfield ignored them. Guiteau went on, "This is not murder. It is a political necessity. It will make my friend Arthur President."

PRESIDENTIAL VACATION

Despite Lucretia's progress in regaining her strength, Boynton recommended a change in scenery. He suggested to Garfield that his wife would have a speedier recovery in the cool sea breezes of New Jersey away from the stifling heat and humidity of Washington. The Garfields made plans to vacation at a hotel in the Elberon section of Long Branch, a beach resort town visited by both Presidents Grant and Hayes.

On the morning of June 18, Garfield, his wife, the three youngest children, the Boyntons, and a close friend set out from the White House to Washington's Baltimore and Potomac Depot to board a train for New Jersey. They expected the journey to take until the end of the day.

Charles Guiteau had paid attention to the president's activities, waiting for the right time to fulfill his "destiny . . . to obey the divine will." When he read about the Garfields' vacation, he made sure he was at the train depot Saturday morning. Armed with his loaded gun, he intended to kill the president that day.

But once he saw the group, Guiteau changed his mind. Lucretia seemed too pale and weak. He had met her several weeks before at a White House reception open to the public. She had been friendly, and he liked her. During her illness, he'd felt sympathy for her. He'd sent his wishes for her recovery in two of his many letters to the president, all of which were intercepted by White House staff before reaching Garfield.

Guiteau couldn't shoot. "Mrs. Garfield looked so thin and clung so tenderly to the President's arm," he wrote later that day, "my heart failed me to part them, and I decided to take him alone."

THE EVENING STROLL

After a pleasant week at the New Jersey shore with Lucretia and his family and friends, James Garfield returned to Washington on Monday, June 27, leaving Lucretia and the children in Elberon.

Alerted by newspaper articles, Charles Guiteau was at the station when Garfield's train pulled in. Sitting in the ladies' waiting room, he watched as the president was greeted by his son and another man, walked to a carriage, and climbed in. Guiteau had a chance to shoot, but once again, he decided the moment wasn't right.

Robert Todd Lincoln (1843–1926), son of Abraham and Mary Todd Lincoln, about the time he was part of the Garfield administration. The night of President Lincoln's assassination, he rushed from the White House to his father's deathbed. During his career, Lincoln served as secretary of war, minister to the United Kingdom, lawyer, and businessman.

Back in the White House, James Garfield went to work. Because he'd been away from his office for several days, he had to spend a busy week catching up on presidential duties.

That Thursday evening, he attended a small dinner at the home of Secretary of the Navy William Hunt. One of the other guests was Secretary of War Robert Todd Lincoln. During the course of the evening, Lincoln talked in detail about the night his father had been assassinated.

Garfield hadn't concerned himself with assassination risks, though he received some death threats by mail during his campaign. In a letter he wrote a week after his election in November 1880, he told a colleague who was anxious about his safety, "Assassination can no more be guarded against than death by lightning; and it is not best to worry about either."

After the meal, Garfield returned to the White House at eleven, wrote in his diary, and went to bed at midnight.

The next day, he sent letters and appointed about two dozen men to diplomatic positions. With those obligations fulfilled, Garfield felt free to anticipate the beginning of a longer vacation with his family. Congress didn't meet during the summer, and the pace of government slowed down.

His itinerary included taking the train to New York the following morning, July 2. This time, his oldest two sons, Hal and Jim, would go with

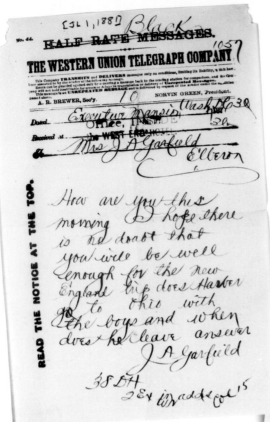

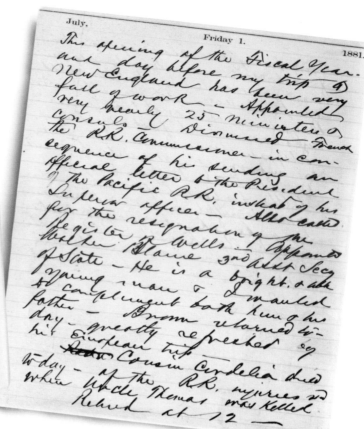

On Friday, July 1, 1881, James Garfield sent this telegram to his wife in Elberon on the New Jersey coast. In it, he finalizes his plans for his New England trip and expresses his hope that Lucretia will feel well enough to go along.

After midnight on July 1, 1881, Garfield recorded his activities of the day: appointing about two dozen diplomats; firing a railroad commissioner; welcoming back his personal secretary, Joseph Stanley Brown, who had been traveling in Europe; and receiving news of his cousin's death. This would be Garfield's final diary entry.

him. Garfield hoped Lucretia would be strong enough to join them after her seashore rest, bringing their daughter Mollie with her.

From there, the family had arranged to visit Williams College in Massachusetts for Garfield's class reunion and to initiate the enrollment of Hal and Jim in fall classes. Then the family would continue on a trip through New England with friends, cabinet members, and their wives.

Meanwhile, the two youngest Garfield boys, Irv and Abe, would travel by train to stay with Ohio relatives. Later in the summer, the entire family planned to reunite for several weeks at the Mentor farm.

When Garfield finished his work on Friday, he decided to stop by Secretary James Blaine's home a couple of blocks away. The weather was fair and in the midseventies—perfect conditions for a walk.

As the president strolled from the White House grounds, one man took notice. Charles Guiteau sat on his regular bench in Lafayette Park, armed with his loaded pistol. When he spotted the president, Guiteau followed him to the Blaine house, hanging several yards back on the opposite sidewalk so that Garfield didn't see him.

Because the secretary wasn't available yet, Garfield chatted with Blaine's wife, Harriet. He had brought along a bound, autographed version of his inaugural speech as a gift to her.

Charles Guiteau waited outside a hotel a half block from Blaine's house, watching for the president to re-emerge. He stepped into the shadows of an alley and checked his gun. He was ready.

After nearly an hour, Garfield and Secretary Blaine exited the house together. The two men walked down the block toward the White House, passing by Guiteau. Engrossed in conversation, they never saw the man lurking on the other side of the street in front of the hotel.

As soon as they'd gone by, Guiteau trailed them as far as the White House gate. He had a clear shot, but he didn't take it. "I felt tired and wearied by the heat," he explained later, "so nothing was done about it then."

Guiteau knew he'd have just one more opportunity before Garfield left the city for the summer. The newspapers reported that the president was beginning his vacation the next morning, July 2. He was scheduled to board the 9:30 train at the Baltimore and Potomac Depot.

Charles Guiteau would be there.

On Friday, July 1, 1881, the morning edition of the *National Republican* newspaper included the itinerary of the president's two-week New England trip. Of interest to Charles Guiteau was the starting date for the trip: Saturday morning.

PERSONAL NOTES.

A BUDGET OF INTERESTING MENTION

The Presidential Excursion—Minister Morton—Minister Thornton's Leave-Taking—Pennsylvania's Handsome Senator—A Loss to Mr. Starin.

No complete outline of the plan and personnel of the President's New England trip has as yet appeared in print. The date fixed for starting from Washington is Saturday morning, not Saturday evening, and the party in full are as follows: The President, Mrs. Garfield, who will join him from Long Branch; their two elder sons, Harry and James; Miss Mollie Garfield, their daughter, who is now with her mother; Colonel and Mrs. Rockwell, with Don Rockwell, their son, and Miss Lulu Rockwell, their daughter; Dr.

The Baltimore and Potomac Depot was completed in 1873. The first floor of the brick building included waiting rooms and a restaurant. Railroad employees used upstairs rooms. The station was torn down in 1908. The National Gallery of Art now occupies the site.

CHAPTER SEVEN
RENDEZVOUS WITH HISTORY

"I had no ill-will toward the President."

—Charles Guiteau

O N THE NIGHT OF JULY 1, CHARLES GUITEAU BOOKED A ROOM at the Riggs House, the same luxury hotel where James Garfield stayed before his inauguration. Guiteau didn't plan to pay for the room or his breakfast the next day.

Waking at about 5:00 a.m. on Saturday, he went for a short stroll to enjoy the morning air. The day promised to be sunny and pleasant. Guiteau stopped by Lafayette Park, where he had spent many hours watching the White House. But Guiteau wasn't waiting for the president. He had already decided where and when to make his move.

PREPARATIONS

After eating breakfast at the Riggs, Guiteau returned to his room to get his gun and important papers. He intended these items to go to the State Department's library. After he disposed of the president, they would be historical treasures.

Among the papers were news clippings, a letter to the press, and the unsent letter he had written on June 16 in which he justified his actions to the American people as "a political necessity." He ended that letter with "I expect President Arthur and Senator Conkling will give the Nation the finest administration it has ever had. They are honest and have plenty of brains and experience."

Guiteau placed an envelope in his side pocket. It contained his "Garfield Against Hancock" speech along with a letter to the White House that he had composed earlier that morning. The letter explained that "the President's tragic death was a sad necessity, but it will unite the Republican party and save the Republic." At the end, Guiteau added, "I am going to the jail."

He anticipated that the public would initially be angry with him for shooting the president. But he was confident they would eventually praise him for his heroic action. Until then, he might require protection from an angry mob.

To guarantee his safety, Guiteau wrote a message on the back of a blank telegram form. It was addressed to William Tecumseh Sherman, a famous Union Civil War general and the current commanding general of the U.S. Army. "I have just shot the President," the note said. "I shot him several times, as I wished him to go as easily as possible . . . Please order out your troops and take possession of the jail at once." Guiteau put the note into his pocket.

After collecting his papers and pistol, Guiteau made his way to the Baltimore and Potomac train station. He "felt well in body and mind."

With plenty of time to spare before the 9:30 train left Washington, Guiteau paid to have his black boots shined so that he looked his best. Then he negotiated a fare with a carriage driver outside the station to take him to the local cemetery when he was finished with Garfield.

To avoid raising the driver's suspicions, Guiteau didn't mention his true destination near the cemetery—the District of Columbia jail. Earlier in June, Guiteau had ridden a streetcar to the jail to see what it was like, at least from the outside. The jail met with his approval, and he planned to turn himself in there after he completed his task.

"I will be out in a few minutes," he told the carriage driver before going inside the train station, "and when I come out and get into your carriage I want you to drive very fast; I am in a hurry."

After entering the station, Guiteau approached the newsstand next to the ladies' waiting room. He asked the young man in charge if he could leave some papers with him. Guiteau laid down his bundle, tied with a string. Besides the letters he'd written, he left a package for the *New York Herald* that contained his book, *The Truth,* with his suggestion that the newspaper print it. He held on to the envelope for the White House and the note to General Sherman.

Nervously, Guiteau paced up and down the main waiting room, "working myself up," he later said, "as I knew the hour was at hand." He frequently peered through the two doorways into the ladies' waiting room where he saw several people sitting on the benches or standing around. Guiteau expected the president to come through this area because he had seen him use the B Street entrance twice before.

Sarah White, the ladies' waiting room matron, noticed the small man with a short beard and dark clothing occasionally wiping the sweat from his face. Her job was to protect women in the room from unwanted male attention, and she didn't like the way he was loitering close by. She kept her eye on him.

TO THE STATION

James Garfield was in a fine mood that Saturday morning. He would soon see Lucretia, and his vacation meant a break from the tedious business of politics and office seekers.

When Hal and Jim awoke, the president playfully roughhoused with them. Fifteen-year-old Jim did a handspring over the bed and dared his father to do one, too. Laughing, Garfield copied his son.

After breakfast, Secretary of State Blaine arrived at the White House. The night before, he and Garfield discussed business until nearly midnight. They agreed that Blaine should meet the president again in the morning in order to review final details that might need attention during Garfield's absence.

As the president prepared to depart for the train station, the two men talked for a few minutes. On their way from the White House, they stopped by Joseph Stanley Brown's office. Smiling as he clasped his secretary's hand, Garfield said, "You have had your holiday, now I am going to have mine."

Then he and Blaine went outside and got into Blaine's carriage for the ride to the station, a little more than a mile away. Hal and Jim rode behind them in the Garfields' carriage. The rest of the presidential group making the trip north were to meet them at the train.

Outside the station, Garfield and Blaine pulled up to the B Street entrance. Police Officer Patrick Kearney stood nearby. He recognized the man in the light gray suit as President Garfield.

"How much time have I got?" Garfield asked him from the carriage.

Kearney walked over, took out his watch, and showed it to the president. With about ten minutes until the 9:30 train left, Garfield and Blaine sat in the carriage a bit longer, finishing their conversation. Then they climbed out and went up the B Street entrance stairs toward the ladies' waiting room.

THE NECESSARY DEED

Guiteau checked the station clock. It was 9:20. The president would be arriving soon. He stepped into the ladies' waiting room and stood near the street entrance. From there, he watched the carriage pull up outside.

The president wasn't alone. Guiteau recognized the secretary of state. But

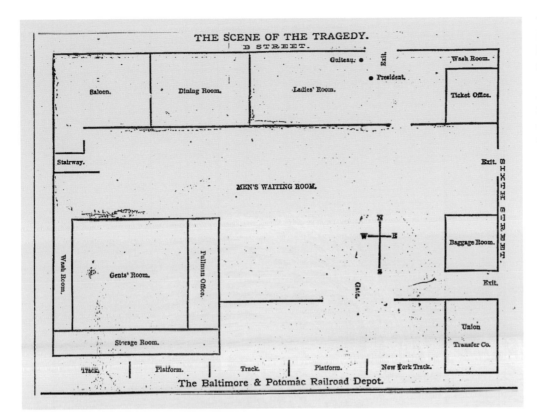

THE SCENE OF THE TRAGEDY.

B STREET.

Guiteau ●   Exit.   Wash Room.

● President.

Saloon.   Dining Room.   Ladies' Room.   Ticket Office.

Stairway.   Exit.   SIXTH STREET

MEN'S WAITING ROOM.

N
W — E
S

Wash Room.   Gents' Room.   Pullman Office.   Baggage Room.

Gate.   Exit.

Storage Room.   Union Transfer Co.

Track.   Platform.   Track.   Platform.   New York Track.

The Baltimore & Potomac Railroad Depot.

This diagram of the Baltimore and Potomac Depot appeared in the *Chicago Tribune* on July 3, 1881. It shows the B Street and Sixth Street exits and the position of Guiteau and the president during the shooting. Garfield and Blaine had been walking from the B Street door toward the gate, where the president was to board the train. The room labeled "Men's Waiting Room" was the station's main waiting room.

that wasn't going to change his plan. Guiteau ignored Blaine. It was Garfield he was after. It was Garfield who had to pay.

As Garfield and Blaine entered the ladies' waiting room, neither man noticed Guiteau standing to their right. With Blaine slightly ahead, they passed between the benches and walked toward the main waiting room.

Guiteau moved forward until he was about six feet from Garfield. He drew out his gun, extended his arm, aimed at the president's back, and pulled the trigger. Advancing closer, he shot again.

Blaine heard a sudden loud bang to his right. His first thought was that a gun had been fired in the station and "there might be some danger . . . [from] stray bullets flying around." He touched Garfield's arm to speed him along to safety.

Garfield turned toward the sound. "My God! What is this?" he cried, throwing up his hands.

This 1881 print illustrates the moment Charles Guiteau shot the president in the ladies' waiting room at the Baltimore and Potomac Depot on July 2. Secretary Blaine and several witnesses look on. The ladies' waiting room matron, Sarah White, stands to the left. According to her, few people were in the room at the time of the shooting. The illustration shows Blaine looking directly at Guiteau. But Blaine said that he only saw the side of Guiteau's face as the man passed him seconds after the shooting.

At that moment, Blaine heard the second gunshot. A man brushed past him. Without thinking, Blaine followed.

The two gunshots echoed through the station. People screamed and shouted.

When Sarah White, the ladies' waiting room matron, heard the first shot, she glanced over. The shooter stood less than a yard behind the president, firing again. It was the same suspicious man she'd seen earlier that morning.

President Garfield fell to his knees, then collapsed to the floor on his back. White circled the benches to reach him. Dropping down, she lifted his head up and rested it in her lap.

"LYNCH HIM!"

After Guiteau saw the president fall, he pivoted toward the B Street door, shoving the pistol into his right hip pocket. The carriage he'd hired would be waiting outside, ready to take him to the jail.

His exit from the station was blocked by Officer Kearney, who a few minutes before had shown Garfield his watch. When Kearney heard the gunshots, he ran to the door of the ladies' waiting room, where he encountered Guiteau trying to leave. Kearney wasn't about to let anyone out until he learned what was happening.

The officer didn't realize that Guiteau was the shooter, but others did. Within seconds, ticket agent Robert Parke rushed up and took hold of Guiteau's collar. "This is the man that shot the President," Parke called out.

Police officer John Scott, assigned to the train station, sprinted across the large main waiting room to help Parke.

Scott grabbed Guiteau's arm, and Officer Kearney seized him, too.

Secretary Blaine had taken several steps in pursuit of the shooter when he heard the shout, "We have got him; we have caught him." He recognized the scrawny man they held. Charles Guiteau.

Guiteau waved a piece of paper in his hand. He kept repeating, "I want this letter delivered to General Sherman."

As Officers Kearney and Scott dragged Guiteau out the Sixth Street door, some men inside the station yelled, "Lynch him!"

When they got outside, Guiteau told the two officers, "I did it, and will go to jail for it. Arthur is President, and I am a stalwart."

After handing the shooter over to the police officers, ticket agent Robert Parke crossed the ladies' waiting room to the fallen president. Bending down next to Sarah White, he took off Garfield's tie and unbuttoned his collar.

CHECKING FOR INJURY

Garfield's two sons had arrived at the station in the carriage behind their father. After he and Secretary Blaine entered the station, their carriage pulled up to the entrance. Just as the brothers were about to go inside, they heard two shots.

They raced into the ladies' waiting room and saw their father on the floor with Secretary Blaine standing over him. A woman held Garfield's head in her lap. The boys weren't sure whether their papa was alive or dead.

"I was frightened and could do nothing but cry," Jim admitted in his diary later that day.

Dr. Smith Townshend was Washington's health officer. He was in his office near the station when someone dashed in to alert him about the attack on the president. Townshend hurried to the railroad depot, arriving within five minutes of the shooting.

He stooped down to examine Garfield. The president was alive but had symptoms of shock. His face was ashen, his pulse was faint, and he had vomited and then fainted. His head had been raised too high by someone trying to help. Townshend lowered it so that the president's legs were above the level of his head and blood could flow to his brain and other organs.

To bring Garfield from the faint, the doctor gave him smelling salts and brandy. Today we know that an alcoholic beverage like brandy shouldn't be

A gold star was later placed on the spot where James Garfield fell, and a wall plaque commemorated the shooting.

given to a person in shock. At that time, however, it was considered a way to revive and stimulate a patient.

Once Garfield was conscious again, Townshend asked, Are you in pain?

The president replied that he felt a prickling sensation in his right foot and leg.

Townshend suspected this was a sign of damage to the spine. Can you turn over? he asked.

Garfield said he could, and turned onto his side.

People in the room told Townshend there had been two shots. He pulled up Garfield's bloody clothing and scanned his back. The doctor spotted blood seeping from an entry wound on the right side, near the waist about four inches from the backbone. Using his finger, Townshend removed a small blood clot at the opening where the bullet had entered. He checked over the body for evidence of a second wound but couldn't find any.

What Townshend didn't know was that the first bullet grazed Garfield's upper right arm, leaving a minor flesh wound. Nearly two weeks later, a laborer who had been in the station discovered that the bullet had penetrated his work kit and fallen inside it.

Turning Garfield onto his back again, Townshend feared the worst. It looked as if the president was mortally wounded.

What's your opinion? Garfield asked him.

Townshend replied with encouraging words, trying not to show his pessimism.

Garfield wasn't fooled. "Doctor, I am a dead man."

CHAPTER EIGHT
IN SHOCK

"In many cases the best probe is the surgeon's finger."

—Dr. S. D. Gross, *A Manual of Military Surgery*, 1861

"The finger is the proper probe."

—Dr. J. Julian Chicolm, *A Manual of Military Surgery*, 1861

THE PRESIDENT LAY ON THE WAITING ROOM FLOOR, WHERE DOZENS of people had walked that day, their shoes and boots carrying soot, dirt, and horse manure from the street. With a crowd gathering and the president vomiting, Dr. Smith Townshend called for help in carrying Garfield to a more private area.

Station employees brought a coarse mattress from a nearby sleeping car. Garfield was gently lifted onto it and carried up the stairs to a large room on the station's second story. Following behind were his sons, friends, and several cabinet members who had been at the station.

Garfield seemed exhausted by the move, and Dr. Townshend gave him additional brandy to stimulate him. Seventeen-year-old Hal knelt beside his father, holding back tears and trying to be brave. Now more alert than he had been downstairs, Garfield spoke calming words to his son.

When the shots were fired, the president's aide and his friend since college, Colonel Almon Rockwell, was in the station ready to accompany the Garfields on their summer trip. He rushed to the president's side. Garfield asked him to immediately send a telegram to Lucretia, who was still in New Jersey preparing to join her husband later in the day. "The President wishes me to say to you from him that he has been seriously hurt. How seriously he cannot yet say. He is himself, and hopes you will come to him soon. He sends his love to you." The news reached her twenty minutes after the shooting.

"THE PRESIDENT IS SHOT!"

Secretary of War Robert Todd Lincoln had been invited to accompany Garfield on his vacation trip, but he was forced to delay his departure by a day. On Saturday morning, he came to the station to tell the president that he'd be joining the group later. As he entered the building, someone yelled that the president had been shot.

Lincoln sprinted ahead and saw Garfield on the floor of the ladies' waiting room with his eyes closed, surrounded by several people. Quickly assessing the situation, Lincoln ran back to his carriage and sent the driver to fetch his friend Dr. D. W. Bliss. Bliss had been a surgeon for thirty years and was considered an expert in gunshot wounds.

News of the shooting had already spread—by telegraph, telephone, and word of mouth. A policeman on horseback rode through Washington's streets calling, "The President is shot! The President is shot!"

Dr. Charles Purvis was walking a couple of blocks from the station when he heard that the president had been wounded. One of the few African American doctors in Washington, Purvis was a surgeon at the Freedmen's Hospital. Within minutes, he had climbed the station's staircase to the second floor, where Garfield lay on a mattress in the corner of the room. Purvis was the second doctor at the scene.

He looked at the injury but didn't touch it. Purvis noted that the president's breathing was weak and his skin pale and clammy. Recognizing that Garfield was in shock, he covered him with blankets and sent for bottles of hot water to put at his feet to warm him. Then he gave the president more brandy.

Soon other doctors showed up. Some were government officials, including the city's coroner and the surgeons general of the Navy and the Marine Hospital Service. Others were physicians who happened to be close by and came to offer whatever help they could.

Responding to Lincoln's request, Dr. Bliss got to the station about twenty minutes after the shooting. He found Garfield lying on his left side with his coat removed and his blood-soaked shirt pulled up to expose the wound.

Without hesitating, Bliss took over. He checked the injury himself, sticking his little finger into the opening to feel if the bullet was near the surface. A former Civil War surgeon, he was following the procedure recommended in military surgery manuals used by both Union and Confederate doctors. Like Townshend, he had not washed his hands.

Dr. D. W. Bliss (1825–1889). During the Civil War, when this photograph was taken, Bliss served as chief surgeon of a large U.S. Army hospital in Washington. In 1881, he was a practicing surgeon, considered an expert on treating gunshot wounds.

With his finger, Bliss detected a broken rib but no bullet. Then, one at a time, he inserted two different metal probes about three inches deep into the wound, moving each around inside Garfield's body in an attempt to locate the bullet. These instruments were not washed or sterilized.

Without X-rays (not yet invented), the only way to find a bullet was by probing for it. Doctors hoped it was within reach of the entry wound and could be easily pulled out with their instruments. Bliss concluded the bullet had gone deep.

Lincoln stood to the side watching the examination. Though he knew the probing must be excruciating for the president, Garfield seemed to be "the coolest man in the room, telling in a clear strong voice the location of his pains in answer to the surgeons."

Garfield asked Bliss how serious the injury was. The doctor said he didn't know yet. He held back what he really thought. The wound looked fatal.

The president replied that he wanted to be moved to the White House. Bliss conferred with the nine other doctors in the room. No one was optimistic about Garfield's chances of survival. They agreed he should be taken home for treatment and, possibly, to die. In either case, a hospital was out of the question. The president would receive better care at the White House than in a crowded hospital, which was generally for people with no one to nurse them at home.

TO THE WHITE HOUSE

After an agonizing hour of doctors poking and prodding, eight men carried Garfield on the mattress through the train station to the exit. They eased him into the back of a horse-drawn ambulance and onto a pile of mattresses removed from a train car and put there to absorb the jolts. Surrounded by policemen on horses, the ambulance sped down Pennsylvania Avenue to the White House.

A messenger on horseback had ridden ahead to announce to the White House staff that the president had been shot and was on his way. Stunned, Joseph Stanley Brown pulled himself together and instructed the steward to fix up a bedroom. Then he telegraphed the chief of the city's police to send officers to the White House to protect it.

Harriet Blaine was eating breakfast, waiting for her husband to return home from the train station. A servant ran in with the news "that the President is assassinated." Knowing her husband had been with Garfield, Harriet was afraid that Blaine had been shot, too. Without delay, she took a carriage the short distance to the White House. The streets were in turmoil, with people and carriages racing about. She saw policemen clearing the way for the ambulance.

When Harriet arrived at the White House, she learned that her husband was safe. She waited in the hall for Garfield to be brought in. A group of men entered, carrying him on a mattress. She followed as they took him into a bedroom and carefully lowered him onto a bed. Garfield caught her eye, and Harriet stepped over to him. "Whatever happens," he said, "I want you to promise to look out for Crete. Don't leave me until Crete comes."

Garfield was placed on his right side so that the bloody discharge could drain from the wound more easily. A temporary dressing was applied, but neither the wound nor the skin around it was cleaned or disinfected.

The president complained of severe pain in his legs, and the doctors gave him morphine. Throughout the day, he received additional injections whenever the pain intensified. He was also given water and brandy. Every half hour, Garfield vomited. His pulse raced.

Dr. Susan Edson, physician for Lucretia and the children, heard of the shooting from her brother and sister, who had been near the train station. She left her home and hurried to the White House, arriving just as the president was brought up to his room.

Garfield asked her to send a telegram to Lucretia. He was concerned that the shock of this news would cause a relapse in his wife's illness. Tell her, he said to Edson, "I am home and as comfortable as possible under the circumstances."

By this time, Lucretia and Mollie were aboard an express train from New Jersey to Washington. The trip would take more than six hours. As the day went on, the president repeatedly asked Edson if they'd heard from Lucretia yet. When was she was expected back? "His greatest anxiety seemed to be for her," Edson recalled, "though his chances for life appeared very few." The doctor was worried that he wouldn't live long enough to see his wife again.

That afternoon, the president asked Secretary of State Blaine who had shot him. When he heard the name, Garfield said, "Why did he do it? What have I done, that this must come to me."

THE ASSASSIN

Within minutes of the shooting, policemen hustled Charles Guiteau from the railroad depot and dragged him two blocks to the police station. Only then did anyone think to go through Guiteau's pockets. They discovered that he still carried the pistol in his hip pocket. Officers also confiscated the knife he bought at the same time as the gun, a stack of his name cards, the envelope intended for the White House, some folded newspaper clippings about Garfield and Conkling, and twenty cents.

"You stick to me," Guiteau told one of the officers. "Arthur and all those men are my friends, and I'll have you made Chief of Police."

When he was informed that Garfield was still alive, Guiteau said, "I wish I had given him the third bullet, and put him out of his misery."

General Sherman, who was not at the train station, never received the note Guiteau intended for him. But when the general heard about the attempt on the president's life, he ordered troops into the streets and to the White House. Sherman wanted to be prepared in case

Charles Guiteau in the District of Columbia jail in an illustration from a book published about the shooting.

the shooting was part of a broader conspiracy the way the Lincoln assassination had been.

As the wounded Garfield was being transferred to the White House by ambulance, police were driving the handcuffed Guiteau to the District of Columbia jail, the same one he had visited. Sherman sent soldiers to guard the jail and protect the shooter from the angry crowd, just as Guiteau asked the general to do in his undelivered note.

BREAKING BULLETINS

Telegraphed messages swept across the nation within the hour. Garfield is shot. The assassin is in jail. Shocked and in despair, people couldn't believe it had happened again to one of their presidents.

Reporters flocked to the White House. Starting in late morning, the staff released regular updates about Garfield. Brown gave passes to journalists so that they had access to officials in the building. He decided the public had a right to know what was happening with their president.

The White House reporters interviewed visitors, including doctors who had been in to see the president. They also talked to cabinet members, their wives, and the Garfields' friends.

Other journalists questioned policemen and people at the train station. They went to the jail to meet with the assassin, though officials turned them away. When word got out that Guiteau was originally from Chicago, reporters in that city dug into his past, interviewing those who had known him. A picture emerged of an unstable deadbeat, swindler, and failed lawyer and lecturer.

Newspapers all over the country posted the latest news outside their offices. Crowds converged around these bulletin boards as people anxiously awaited updates on Garfield's condition. The first bulletins said that he was dead. Next they said he was alive but gravely wounded.

Headlines shout news of the shooting: *Chicago Tribune* (left). *New York Sun* (middle). *Evening Star* [Washington, DC] (top right). *Sunday Globe* [St. Paul, MN] (bottom right).

THE PEOPLE.

How the News of Black Saturday Fell upon Them.

A Cry of Horror Went Up from Maine to California.

Meetings of Grief-Stricken People Throughout the United States.

Fourth of July Celebrations Turned to Pageants of Grief and Gloom.

Scenes in the Metropolis After the Reception of the News.

Unaffected Consternation of Arthur upon Reading the Telegram.

The Poor Old People at Mentor —The President's Mother Yet Uninformed.

Chicago Stricken with Sorrow and Horror to the Heart's Core.

The News Received with Every Manifestation of Deep Grief.

Thronging Crowds Besieging "The Tribune" Office Eager for News.

The Shouts of Joyful Relief When "There Is Hope!" Was Bulletined.

Opinions of Senator Logan, Congressman Davis, E. A. Storrs, and Many Others.

Resolutions of the North American Saengerbund—Henry Villard and Henry Watterson.

THE PRESIDENT SHOT.

A Mortal Wound from an Assassin's Hand.

Fired On in a Washington Railroad Depot.

Arrest of the Murderer Charles Guiteau.

THE MAN SAID TO BE INSANE.

Mrs. Garfield Hurries to Her Husband's Bedside.

The Vice-President on his Way at Midnight to the Capital.

A Deed that has Filled the Country with Horror.

TWO SHOTS FIRED.

ARREST OF THE ASSASSIN.

THE CITY HORRIFIED.

ASSASSIN'S WORK!

GARFIELD SHOT.

BY CHICAGO LUNATIC!

President Still Living.

And Slight Hopes Entertained

His Life Hangs on Slender Thread

C. GUITEAU, THE ASSASSIN

DETAILS OF THE TERRIBLE AFFAIR.

In major cities, newspapers printed extra editions as more details surfaced. Headlines screamed: "Garfield Shot Twice by a Disappointed Office Seeker"; "A Cry of Horror Went Up from Maine to California"; "His Life Hangs on Slender Thread."

Many of the news articles published hastily that day were inaccurate. In the confusion, reports conflicted. The public wasn't sure what the truth was.

Garfield's mother was in Ohio visiting her daughters, and they shielded her from the news reports until they knew more about his condition. The two youngest Garfield boys, ages ten and eight, were traveling by train from New Jersey to Ohio. They weren't told of the shooting until they reached Lucretia's family at the Mentor Farm.

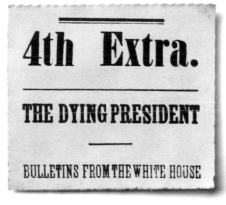

4th Extra.

THE DYING PRESIDENT

BULLETINS FROM THE WHITE HOUSE

Many newspapers in large cities printed several editions on July 2, updating their articles as new developments unfolded. By the end of the day, the *Evening Star* reported that Garfield was dying.

HOPE FADES

By late afternoon, some news reports claimed that Garfield had passed away. In fact, though he wasn't dead, he had grown weaker as the day continued.

When Hal and Jim welcomed their mother and sister back from New Jersey in early evening, Jim realized that "all hope was given up . . . Papa was expected to die within an hour at 7."

Lucretia immediately went to Garfield's bedside and stayed alone with him for about fifteen minutes. When she came out of the room, Jim was struck by how "very brave & courageous" his mother was.

Fourteen-year-old Mollie entered the bedroom next. "We are so glad to get home and find you as well as you are," she said as cheerfully as she could.

"You are a brave, darling daughter," Garfield replied.

With Papa clinging to life, Jim also sat with his father. "The upper story was not hurt," Garfield said, "it was the hull." He told Jim to "keep up [your] pluck."

Although Garfield remained upbeat with his family, his doctors were discouraged. On Saturday evening, a group of eight physicians, most of whom had been at the train station, reconvened to discuss the case. Garfield's heart was racing, he struggled with each breath, he'd been vomiting every half hour, and he had severe pain in his feet.

Earlier in the day, the doctors had been reluctant to probe the wound again to learn the bullet's path. Knowing that the procedure would be painful, they didn't want to disturb Garfield while he was in such a fragile state.

But that evening, they agreed they needed more information about the injury so that they could decide how to handle it. Bliss asked Surgeon General of the Navy Philip Wales to perform the exam. With the president lying on his left side, Wales stuck his little finger into the wound as far as he could. He announced to the other doctors that he felt two fractured ribs and a one-inch-deep cut in the liver.

Many of these physicians had served as surgeons during the Civil War, and they had seen men die from battlefield gunshots. They didn't know where the bullet was, but the evidence indicated it had damaged the liver and perhaps other organs. The doctors believed Garfield was bleeding internally.

Surgical techniques then weren't effective or safe enough to search blindly for a bullet deep in the body or to repair vital organs. The only treatment was to relieve the president's pain and nausea, keep him warm, and ensure that he rested with "absolute quiet."

At 8:30 that night, a fresh dressing was put on his wound. His remaining clothes were cut away, carefully, so as not to cause him more discomfort. Since the shooting, he'd been wearing the same clothing, bloody and dirty from lying on the station floor.

James Garfield closed his eyes and drifted off to sleep. Nobody expected him to survive the night.

VOL. IX.—No. 226.

JULY 6, 1881.

Puck

The shooting of Garfield was *Puck* magazine's cover story on July 6, 1881. The illustration shows the president guiding the ship of state [the nation] among high waves. He had been heading the ship toward "Good Government" when he was attacked. The caption to the image reads "Struck Down at the Post of Duty."

THE ILLUSTRATED LONDON NEWS

REGISTERED AT THE GENERAL POST-OFFICE FOR TRANSMISSION ABROAD.

No. 2204.—VOL. LXXIX.   SATURDAY, AUGUST 13, 1881.   WITH TWO SUPPLEMENTS } SIXPENCE. By Post, 6½D.

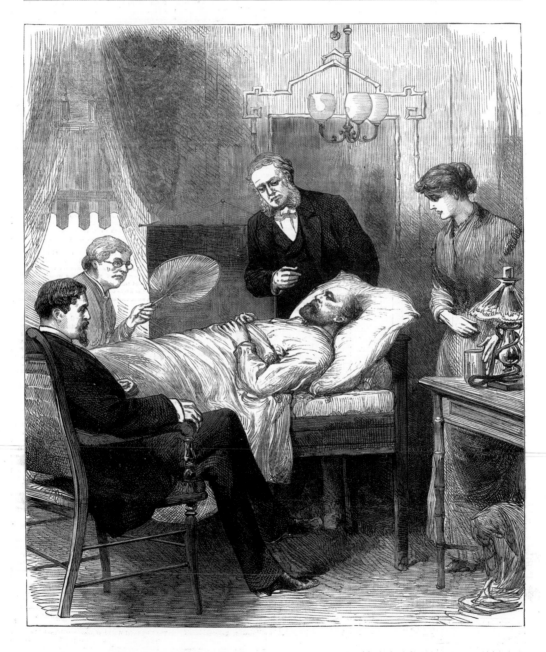

Illustrations of Garfield's sickroom appeared in several news magazines during the summer of 1881. This was sketched by an artist allowed to stand outside the room. Before photographs were printed in newspapers and magazines, sketch artists created images of important scenes. Surrounding Garfield are Dr. Susan Edson with the fan, Dr. D. W. Bliss and Lucretia at the head of the bed, and Garfield's friend David Swaim in the chair.

CHAPTER NINE
UNCERTAINTY

"If I can't save him, no one can."

—Dr. D. W. Bliss

URING THE NIGHT, GARFIELD CONTINUED TO vomit every half hour. The tingling and pain in his feet hadn't disappeared, and the doctors guessed that his spinal cord was damaged. They gave him morphine to dull the discomfort and help him sleep. Although his heart rate was still too high, his temperature and breathing became normal.

When Garfield awoke on Sunday morning, he was calm and positive, just as he had been the day before, even joking with people around him. He asked Dr. Bliss about his chances of surviving his wound.

Bliss responded, "Your injury is formidable. In my judgment, you have a chance for recovery."

Smiling, Garfield put his hand on Bliss's arm. "Well, Doctor, we'll take that chance."

HE STILL LIVES !

The President Promises to Foil the Assassin.

STORY OF THE CRIME AND THE CRIMINAL'S CAPTURE.

Excitement in the City and Threats of Lynching.

The headline from the *Washington Post* on July 3, 1881, the morning after the assassination attempt

Lucretia Garfield took Bliss aside and requested that he be honest with her about her husband's condition. She made clear that, as Christians, she and James were prepared to accept God's will. The doctor promised to keep her informed.

Lucretia was unaware that a controversy was already brewing about Bliss's treatment of the president.

DOCTOR DISPUTE

Early Sunday morning, Garfield's regular Washington physician, Dr. Jedediah Baxter, came back to the capital from a trip to Pennsylvania. Concerned about his patient, he went directly to the White House. Bliss refused to let him into the sickroom, claiming that Baxter would disturb Garfield.

When Baxter protested, Bliss became angry and insulting. Barred from visiting Garfield, Baxter left, never able to return to the president's side again. He publicly charged that Bliss had broken the American Medical Association's ethical code, which gave a patient's regular doctor the right to see him. After learning of the incident, other physicians agreed with Baxter.

Bliss's actions also troubled the group of Washington doctors who had attended Garfield since the shooting. These men met at the White House on Sunday morning to discuss the president's progress during the night, and they planned to reconvene at the White House that evening. But during the afternoon, each was surprised to receive a letter from Bliss. He thanked them for their help, adding that their assistance was no longer needed. It was best for the president if fewer doctors visited the sickroom.

Bliss claimed that he had chosen his permanent medical staff at the request of the president. Only one doctor from the original group remained on this team—Dr. Robert Reyburn, a friend whom Bliss sent for from the train station immediately after the shooting. The new physicians were Surgeon General Joseph Barnes and Dr. J. J. Woodward from the U.S. Army's surgeon general office, neither of whom regularly treated patients as part of his job.

Some doctors in the first group were upset by the way Bliss pushed them aside, and they shared their displeasure with reporters. One doctor complained, "I am afraid Bliss will probe the wound, and if he does, inflammation will set in and the President will die. Nothing can save him then."

Another asserted that the bullet was inside Garfield's liver, where it would kill him either by infection or bleeding. He gave the president ten days more to live, at the most.

Boynton, Garfield's cousin, was also critical of Bliss. He declared that Garfield's care "was bad at the start" and that the doctor had not properly cleaned out the wound.

Bliss would only allow Boynton and Edson to stay at Garfield's side if they served as nurses. In Bliss's view, the two were disqualified from treating the president because they were homeopaths.

Homeopathy is a type of medicine that rejects the use of harsh chemicals and other techniques. In 1881, many traditional doctors considered homeopaths to be quacks employing useless and sometimes dangerous medicines. Boynton and Edson, however, believed their medicinal remedies were safer and more effective.

Bliss had shut out the three physicians with the closest ties to the Garfield family—Baxter, Boynton, and Edson—from all decisions concerning the president's treatment. When anyone questioned his authority, Bliss claimed that the Garfields asked him to supervise the care. Months later, Boynton accused him of lying, telling a medical journal that "neither the President nor Mrs. Garfield ever asked him to take charge of the case."

PRESIDENTIAL CARE

Bliss decided on the medications and food the president received. Drs. Reyburn and Woodward measured Garfield's temperature, breathing rate, and pulse

three times a day and took turns spending the night at the White House. They kept notes on the case, which were used to write the daily bulletins issued to the press. Surgeon General Barnes came to the White House twice a day to assess Garfield's condition and discuss it with the other three doctors.

The president was bedridden and incapacitated. His care involved feeding him, changing his clothes and sheets, cleaning him up like a baby after he urinated and defecated, keeping him company, and reading to him. The weather outside was hot and the room even hotter. Someone usually sat beside the bed fanning Garfield and giving him ice chips to suck.

To prevent bedsores, his attendants shifted his position multiple times a day. Because of Garfield's size, this required the efforts of several people.

Nursing duties were shared by Boynton; Edson; the White House steward, William Crump; Almon Rockwell, who had studied medicine; and General David Swaim, who was Garfield's army friend. At times, the cabinet members' wives assisted.

Throughout Garfield's ordeal, at least one of the doctors or these nursing attendants stayed by his side. To avoid disturbing him, they tried to maintain quiet and to limit the number of people in the room to two or three.

James Garfield was a large man, standing over 6 feet and weighing 210 pounds. Changing his position in bed was a challenge for his caregivers.

Lucretia was always nearby, reluctant to leave her husband's bedside. Though she was still fatigued from her bout with malaria, she impressed everyone with her strength and courage as she dealt with Garfield's precarious condition.

POINTING FINGERS

On the day that Garfield was shot, Vice President Chester Arthur had been in New York City with his good friend Roscoe Conkling. Secretary of State Blaine sent Arthur telegrams every few hours with updates on the president's health.

When Garfield seemed near death Saturday evening, Blaine recommended that Arthur return to Washington as soon as possible, and the vice president took the night train out of New York. The shooting shocked Arthur. He never anticipated something like this happening, and he prayed that Garfield would survive.

Within hours of Guiteau's attack, rumors spread, accusing Arthur of participating in a plot to kill Garfield. It didn't help that Guiteau had written down his intent to make his "friend Arthur President."

Less conspiratorial voices pointed at the Stalwarts' harsh criticisms of the president that had provoked a man like Guiteau. Newspaper editorials blamed the assassination attempt on a "narrow and bitter hatred which has been only too freely indulged." In a veiled reference to Conkling and the Stalwarts, the New York Times said, "His [Guiteau's] resentment was inflamed and intensified by the assaults upon the President which have been common in too many circles for the past few months."

The idea of Chester Arthur becoming president alarmed many American voters. They didn't think that his ability, experience, and ethics qualified him. People had voted for James Garfield, never expecting Arthur to inherit the office.

On Sunday morning, with Garfield's fate unknown, former President

Rutherford Hayes wrote in his diary that the country faced a disaster if Garfield died. "Arthur for President! Conkling the power behind the throne, superior to the throne!" Hayes dreaded an administration led by those two.

Since his inauguration as vice president, Arthur had had little contact with Garfield except to lobby for political appointments that the Stalwarts wanted. He remained loyal to Roscoe Conkling, even living with the senator in Washington. Garfield and his allies didn't trust Arthur, and the vice president knew it.

Arthur didn't want to appear eager to take over the presidency, especially in light of the accusations and criticisms of him in the newspapers. He released sincere public statements deploring the shooting and condemning it as evil. He also denied any association with Guiteau other than seeing him on many occasions at New York City's Republican headquarters and a few times on Washington's streets.

Conkling refused to be interviewed. But people remembered his nasty political war with Garfield. Extra police were sent to guard him against several threats on his life.

Early Sunday morning, Vice President Arthur's train arrived in Washington. He sent word to the White House, asking to see Garfield. The doctors turned down his request, and Arthur went to a friend's town house to wait until they would allow a visit. Realizing the sensitive political situation, he avoided the Washington apartment he shared with Conkling.

Later that afternoon, the cabinet, led by Blaine, called on Arthur at the town house. It was a public acknowledgment that Arthur might soon become president and that they all were united behind him.

Sunday evening, Arthur stopped by the White House to pay his respects to Lucretia and express his wishes for Garfield's recovery. He still wasn't permitted to see the president.

THE SPECIALISTS

Although Dr. Bliss rejected the help of several Washington doctors, he sought advice from two nationally respected surgical experts, Philadelphia's D. Hayes Agnew and New York's Frank Hamilton. On Monday morning, July 4, the surgeons arrived at the White House.

Drs. Agnew and Hamilton each examined the bullet wound using probes. They hoped to determine the path that the bullet had taken, which would hint at the internal damage it might have caused. The surgeons couldn't detect the pathway with their probes past a broken rib. Still, they believed the bullet had most likely gone downward into the pelvic region.

Bliss and the original group of doctors had feared that the bullet struck Garfield's internal organs. But based on the president's condition after two days, Agnew and Hamilton believed that no organs had been injured. Garfield had passed urine and feces normally, and neither contained blood. This meant his kidneys and intestines were unharmed. Furthermore, there had been no signs of liver damage, such as severe bleeding. He wasn't paralyzed, indicating that his spinal cord was intact. The doctors attributed the tingling pains in his feet and legs to temporary nerve injury.

Agnew and Hamilton knew from their years practicing military surgery that the human body often encases a bullet in a cyst, or sac, making it harmless. Many Civil War soldiers had lived for years with bullets in their bodies.

Neither doctor thought it wise to cut into Garfield's body to learn more, at least not yet, because he seemed to be holding his own. As long as the bullet wasn't causing problems, they didn't want to create new complications by performing a dangerous operation. Before returning to their home cities, the two surgeons recommended that the current treatment continue.

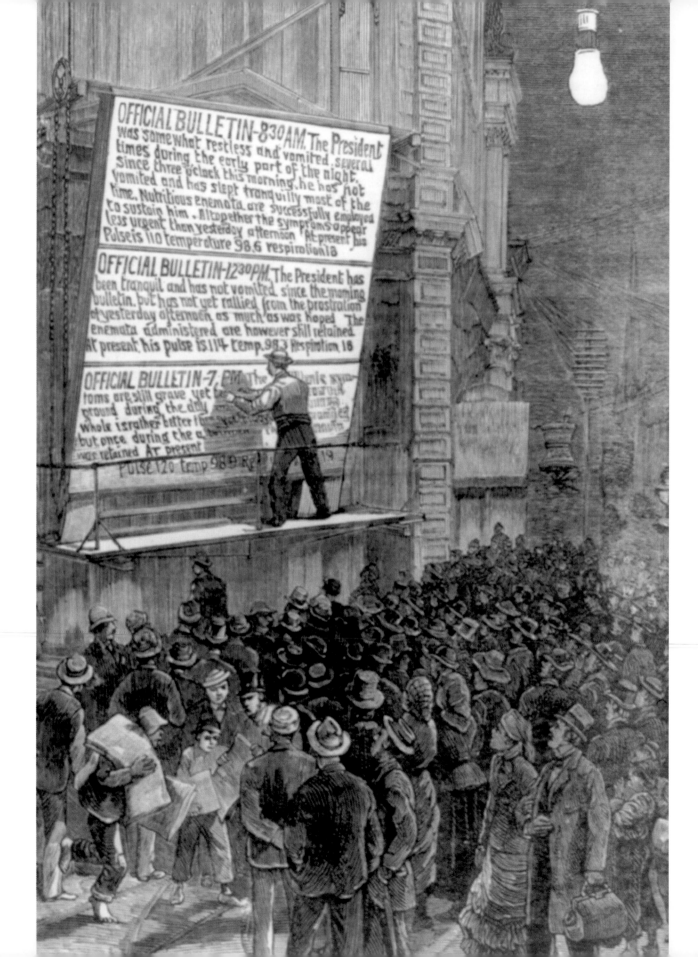

LOVE AND CONCERN

The White House telegraph machine sent out the doctors' medical updates two or three times a day. A worried crowd gathered by the White House gates to hear the latest news.

Worshippers at Sunday services prayed for the president. July Fourth festivities on Monday were subdued as Americans waited to learn whether their president had survived the assassin's bullet.

Residents of the North and South, East and West were saddened and outraged by the assassination attempt. The country was united in concern for Garfield, even though the bitter differences of the Civil War had been slow to disappear.

A newspaper in Richmond, Virginia, the former Confederate capital, lamented "that again has violence attacked the chief executive of the republic . . . a President chosen by the people."

Another Richmond editorial said, "There will in all the earth be no sincerer mourners than the people of the southern section of this Union."

Telegrams and letters from both famous dignitaries and ordinary citizens flooded the White House with heartfelt wishes for Garfield's recovery. Some writers requested a personal update on his condition. One telegram read, "How is our President[?] I am anxious & cannot sleep without knowing."

After one man heard that the president had survived the night, he wrote, "My thanks to kind Providence that your life is spared."

Another note said, "Stick to it Jimmie, I congratulate you upon your pluck."

One telegram sent to General Sherman contained a special message. A military officer asked, "Should the President die may I be the executioner of his assassin[?]"

The public anxiously awaited the details of Garfield's medical condition. As updates came in by telegraph several times a day, newspapers posted them on bulletin boards. This one is at the *New York Herald*. When the report was encouraging, the crowd cheered. When it wasn't, the mood became somber.

PROGRESS

Several days after the shooting, Garfield felt less pain in his feet and was able to get some sleep at night. He could keep down chicken broth, although he occasionally vomited.

Garfield was regularly given morphine injections as well as quinine by mouth. His doctors used quinine as a tonic that would lower his fever and help heal his wounds. The only thing it could do effectively, however, was to treat malaria, which Garfield didn't have. His condition often changed from the doctors' morning bulletin to the evening. Overall, though, the people around him thought he seemed better.

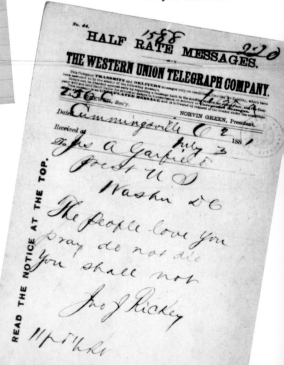

"I congratulate you upon your narrow escape. Let us be thankful to God for having spared you"

"The people love you pray do not die you shall not"

The White House was inundated with telegrams and letters from the public expressing concern for Garfield and offering best wishes. The telegram on the right was sent from a citizen in Cummingsville, Ohio, two days after the shooting. The second came from a man in New York. The stray markings and numbers were added either by the telegraph office or the White House.

When the doctors changed his dressing twice a day, they noticed pus seeping from the bullet wound. Most American physicians considered pus to be a sign that the body was healing itself, and they weren't concerned. They didn't realize that pus was ominous evidence of a bacterial infection.

After the president had been in bed for a week, Bliss decided that he was strong enough for the three oldest children to visit. For the first time since the night of the shooting, Hal, Jim, and Mollie went into the sickroom, each alone. To minimize noise and activity that would sap Garfield's strength, they were warned not to talk to their father or let him talk back.

Garfield couldn't help himself, and he spoke softly to each one. "I guess your papa will pull through," he told Mollie, as she sat by his bedside, "and you will have a papa again."

"Oh yes," she replied, "you are going to get well, I know you will."

STUCK IN JAIL

Charles Guiteau expected to be honored for shooting Garfield. He was certain the public would hail him as a patriot for saving the country. Instead, he was reviled. Newspapers called him "a wretch who represents as distinctly the evil in our system as President GARFIELD represents the good." He was called "a disappointed office-seeker" who "was obviously of disordered mind." One reporter who spotted Guiteau at police headquarters after the shooting described him as "a pale, emaciated, small man, with the appearance of an insane person."

Guiteau's brother-in-law, George Scoville, had just arrived in Washington on business when he learned that his wife's brother had shot the president. Scoville, who was an Illinois lawyer, hurried to the jail to talk to Guiteau. After their meeting, Scoville announced to the newspapers that the man *was* insane and had acted alone, believing he was carrying out God's directions.

Those words made little difference to most Americans. A Virginia newspaper editorial stated that it was fortunate the assassin didn't shoot in the South "for the hot southern blood would have terminated his life without waiting to learn whether he was a maniac or not, (as he was, we take it for granted)." Other articles claimed that Guiteau had carefully planned his attack and was faking insanity.

The police investigation seemed to confirm that Guiteau had no accomplices. That was a relief to the public . . . and also to Arthur and Conkling, who had been accused in the press of conspiring with him.

A grand jury would have to decide if the police had enough evidence to try Guiteau for his crime. But Washington's district attorney, George Corkhill, wasn't ready to take the case before the grand jury. He didn't know yet what crime Guiteau committed. Was it assault with attempt to kill? Or was it murder?

On July 7, five days after the shooting, Corkhill announced that he wouldn't start formal legal action until he learned whether the president lived or died.

The world waited to find out, too.

Charles Guiteau's writings explained his motive for shooting President Garfield. Newspapers and magazines published articles about him, identifying him as a disgruntled office seeker. Guiteau was featured on the cover of *Puck* magazine on July 13, 1881.

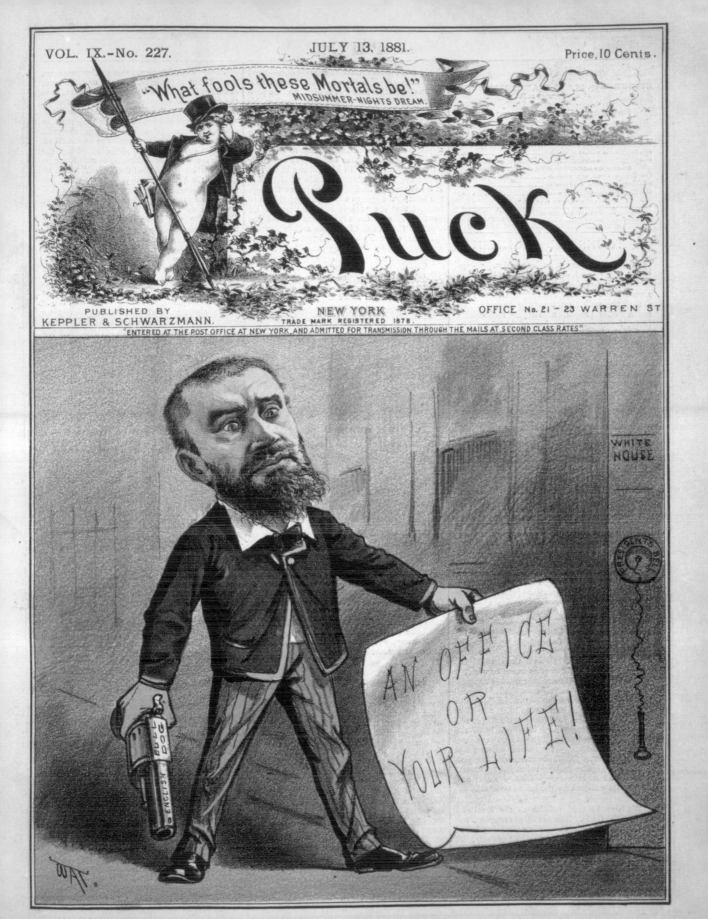

A MODEL OFFICE-SEEKER.

"I am a Lawyer, a Theologian and a Politician!"—*Charles J. Guiteau.*

Beginning the day after the shooting, Dr. D. W. Bliss organized a medical team to handle President Garfield's care. The permanent staff included Drs. Bliss, Reyburn, Barnes, and Woodward. Drs. Agnew and Hamilton were called in as expert surgical consultants. Bliss allowed Drs. Boynton and Edson to provide nursing care only.

D. (David) Hayes Agnew (1818–1892) was a professor of surgery at the University of Pennsylvania Medical School in Philadelphia. He served as a surgeon during the Civil War and was an authority on gunshot wounds. His textbook on surgery was widely respected.

Joseph Barnes (1817–1883) spent his career as a surgeon in the U.S. Army. During the Civil War, he became the U.S. Army's surgeon general, an administrative position he still held at the time of the Garfield shooting. Barnes visited the White House twice a day during the crisis.

D. W. (Doctor Willard) Bliss (1825–1889) practiced surgery in Washington and was considered a gunshot expert because of his Civil War experience. His parents named him after the doctor who attended his birth, Dr. Willard. Although Bliss used his initials, his first and middle names were "Doctor Willard." Bliss and Garfield had known each other since they were teens in Ohio.

Silas Boynton (1835–1907), James Garfield's first cousin and lifelong friend, was trained as a homeopathic doctor. He cared for the Garfield family when they were in Ohio, and he stayed by his cousin's side after the shooting. Boynton did not agree with the treatment Garfield received from the doctors handling his case. He later publicly criticized Bliss.

MEDICAL TEAM

Three of the doctors were also connected to President Lincoln's assassination. In April 1865, Barnes and Bliss were among the several physicians who gathered by the dying president's bed in the boardinghouse across from Ford's Theatre. Woodward helped to perform the autopsy on Lincoln's body at the White House on the day of his death. Barnes was also present for the autopsy.

Susan Edson (1823–1897) was one of the first women to attend an American medical school, studying homeopathic medicine in Cleveland, Ohio. She had her own medical practice until she volunteered her services during the Civil War. Because female doctors were not commissioned as army surgeons, Edson worked as a military nurse. After the war, she practiced medicine in Washington, acting as doctor for Lucretia Garfield and her children when they were in the city.

Frank Hamilton (1813–1886) had a long career as a surgeon, eventually becoming a professor of military surgery at New York City's Bellevue Hospital Medical College. During the Civil War, he served on the battlefield as surgeon for a New York infantry regiment. Later in the war, he acted as one of the Union army's most senior doctors, influencing the surgical treatments of wounded soldiers. Hamilton wrote several textbooks and was regarded as an expert in his field. Bliss knew Hamilton from their war years together.

Robert Reyburn (1833–1909) was a professor of surgery at Howard University in Washington. Bliss sent for him on July 2 immediately after the shooting. Reyburn took turns with J. J. Woodward staying nights at the White House. Reyburn kept the official notes on the president's condition, which were used to make public announcements.

J. J. (Joseph Janvier) Woodward (1833–1884) practiced medicine in Philadelphia until the Civil War began. During the war, he served as a regimental surgeon before beginning duties at the U.S. Army's surgeon general office in Washington. Woodward was assigned to the Army Medical Museum, where he worked until his death, publishing many reports about medicine. He specialized in the medical use of microscopes and photography. He was not an expert on gunshot wounds.

HARPER'S WEEKLY.
JOURNAL OF CIVILIZATION.

VOL. XXV.—No. 1282.
Copyright, 1881, by HARPER & BROTHERS.

NEW YORK, SATURDAY, JULY 23, 1881.

TEN CENTS A COPY.
$4.00 PER YEAR, IN ADVANCE.

JAMES A. GARFIELD.

CHAPTER TEN
"THE NATION'S PATIENT"

"There never was a little girl that was more sorry to hear that
you had been shot, than Your little friend Kate Sprague"

—Kate Sprague, age ten, Jamestown, New York

D URING THE TWO WEEKS AFTER THE SHOOTING, GARFIELD'S
doctors reported that he made steady, slow improvement. His temperature was
slightly elevated, especially late in the day, though the doctors thought it was
nothing to worry about. They gave him daily doses of morphine and quinine.

Garfield's wound continued discharging "healthy pus" through a drainage tube, which
the Bliss team interpreted as a sign of healing. Today, a physician would recognize that fever
and a pus-producing wound pointed to a serious infection.

In its first regular edition to come out after the July 2
shooting, *Harper's Weekly* put the president on its cover.

Dr. Bliss kept saying there was no question that the president would recover. The recuperation might take time, but Garfield was a strong and energetic man.

SENDING ARTHUR HOME

The president stayed good-natured despite enduring the painful changes of his wound dressing, the constant monitoring of his vital signs, and the boredom of lying helpless in bed.

Garfield teased the attendants who checked him for fever. When no one had bothered him for a while, he asked, "Isn't it time for 'Old Temperature' to put in an appearance?"

He remained on his back, with his head and shoulders propped up by pillows when he could tolerate the position. Lucretia and others read to him. He didn't have the strength to hold a newspaper open for very long.

One morning, when his dressing was being changed, Garfield asked Dr. Woodward how the wound was healing. "Oh, it's healing splendidly," Woodward replied, "the matter which is coming from it [pus] is healthy, and everything seems to be in your favor."

Maintaining his sense of humor, Garfield commented, "That is good, but that ball will probably come out a good deal slower than it went in."

Because the president appeared to be out of danger, Vice President Arthur returned to his New York home. There was nothing he could do in Washington anyway. Joseph Stanley Brown sent him the daily medical bulletins by telegram.

Bliss hadn't allowed Arthur or the cabinet into the sickroom because, he said, he didn't want Garfield disturbed. Although Arthur left Washington, cabinet members stayed in the city in case they were needed. When issues arose, the cabinet departments handled them without the president's input.

Garfield had intended Secretary of State Blaine to deal with any other pressing government problems that summer during his planned presidential vacation. But Blaine wasn't permitted to speak with him until July 21, nearly three weeks after the shooting. Even then, Bliss relented only because Garfield insisted. The doctor cut the visit short after just six minutes.

COOLING DOWN

During the first days after the shooting, newspapers reported that Garfield's room was sweltering. Often the president ran a fever, and the room's high temperature increased his suffering. Dozens of letters and telegrams poured into the White House with ideas for cooling the room during the hot Washington summer.

One person suggested moving Garfield to a smaller room filled with ice blocks. Several letter writers based their idea on the fact that cold air sinks. They recommended hanging metal buckets of ice from the ceiling. After the air around the buckets cooled and sank, it would lower the temperature around the president's bed.

Some messages included an elaborate diagram of a cooling device and the offer to set it up in the president's room. Machinery companies sent advertisements for equipment that they guaranteed would cool the air.

One idea was promising enough to try. Troughs of ice water were placed around the room. Long strips of cotton fabric were hung over wooden racks so that their lower edges dipped into the water. The icy water moved up the cloth, soaking it. As the water evaporated from fabric, the room was supposed to cool down. Unfortunately, the method didn't lower the room

In this letter, an eight-year-old boy from Alabama says "that the man that shot you ought to be hung." He continues, "I know if you have a little boy like me he is sorry that you are hurt." In fact, Garfield's youngest son, Abram, was eight, too.

111

NEW YORK, JULY, 6TH.

A. 117 PD. 117.
SECRETARY JAMES G. BLAINE,
WASHINGTON.

TO REDUCE THE TEMPERATURE OF THE PRESIDENTS ROOM, I WOULD ADVISE THE USE OF AN AIR PUMP, OR COMPRESSOR, COMPRESSING AIR INTO A SMALL RESERVOIR TO ABOUT ONE HUNDRED POUNDS TO THE SQUARE INCH AND THEN BY ALLOWING IT TO EXPAND NEARLY FREEZING TEMPERATURE CAN BE OBTAINED. THIS IS NO EXPERIMENT, BUT IS IN CONSTANT USE IN WESTERN MINES FOR REDUCING TEMPERATURE. IT CAN BE REGULATED TO GIVE ANY DESIRED TEMPERATURE WITH DRY AIR. THE MACHINERY SHOULD BE PLACED AT SUFFICIENT DISTANCE FROM THE PRESIDENTS ROOM TO PREVENT ANNOYANCE BY NOISE AND THE COOL AIR CONDUCTED IN PIPES TO THE ROOM. THE NAVY YARD MECHANICS OUGHT TO BE ABLE TO PUT THIS IN OPERATION IN THREE HOURS.
EDWARD BATES DORSEY.

85173

temperature enough to bring relief to the president.

Several people sent letters that recommended constructing a small building outside Garfield's window and filling it with ice. A fan would be positioned to blow over

On July 6, mining engineer Edward Bates Dorsey sent Secretary of State Blaine this telegram. It explains how to keep the president's bedroom cool with the same technology used to lower mine temperatures in Nevada. Dorsey was invited to the White House to set up the cooling machine. But because it required a more powerful engine than he could obtain quickly, the device was never used.

the ice, pushing the cold air through a tube that extended up to the window and into the room.

The president's staff tried a similar approach that didn't require an outside structure. They placed a large container of ice in one room of the White House and connected it to the sickroom with tin pipes. No fans pushed the air, however, and by the time the air reached the president, it was no longer cold.

Next, the White House invited a man from Baltimore, R. S. Jennings, to set up a machine he proposed. Jennings used a gas-powered fan to blow cold air from a huge container full of ice water through pipes into Garfield's room. While the device slightly lowered the room temperature, the machine was too noisy and the air too humid.

After none of the machines adequately cooled the room, one of Garfield's doctors contacted Professor Simon Newcomb, a scientist and mathematician who worked for the U. S. Navy. Newcomb worked alongside Director of the Geological Survey, John Wesley Powell, who had engineering training, to find a solution that improved on Jennings's basic design. Then, with help from Jennings, the men set up their machine in the White House basement. By July 11, nine days after the shooting, it was ready to use.

The air blown up into Garfield's room through tubes was cool and dry, and the noise from the engine was nearly eliminated. When it was 95 degrees outside, the machine kept the area around the president's bed at a comfortable 75 degrees.

Throughout the two months that the innovative device operated, it used at least a half-million pounds of ice. The machine would have worked more efficiently if the sickroom's windows had remained closed. But the Garfields wanted them open because they thought fresh air would aid the president's healing.

GIFTS FOR GARFIELD

The medical team continued releasing its bulletins every morning and evening, and sometimes midday. Reporters stationed at the White House picked up additional information. Newspapers everywhere printed the latest details on their front pages.

Besides learning about Garfield's vital signs each day, readers knew when Garfield slept restlessly, how much pain he had, and how often he moved his bowels. The public read about his diet: milk and rum; toast softened in milk;

slivers of woodcock-breast meat. People found out that he had trouble eating without vomiting afterward.

Drs. Boynton and Edson believed that the morphine, quinine, and alcoholic drinks were leading to vomiting. They knew from many years of medical experience with Garfield that he had a history of stomach problems. The medicines made those worse. Bliss and the other doctors ignored their warnings.

Garfield was aware of the contents of the daily medical bulletins. He said to his friend Swaim, "I should think the people would be tired of having me dished up to them in this way."

Far from it. The public was eager for as much news as possible and reacted to it as if the president was a family member.

Realizing that he needed nourishment to heal and regain his strength, Americans sent gifts of food and drink. Special cod oil to prevent vomiting. A case of milk chocolate, good for an invalid's stomach. Bottles of wine to speed the body's recovery. A cow to provide fresh milk daily (put out to graze on the White House lawn). A watermelon from Georgia. A forty-pound turtle shipped by boat from Key West, Florida (apparently to eat). A pair of woodcock freshly killed on a Civil War battlefield in Maryland (in honor of Garfield's Civil War service). Recipes for broth and soup guaranteed to heal the body.

Besides food and beverages, people suggested ointments and tonics, even enclosing advertisements to show the doctors exactly what to buy. A scientist sent a thermometer that he claimed would provide the most accurate body temperature readings. He requested that it be returned when the doctors were through with it. An inventor offered a special invalid chair, although he said he couldn't afford to give it to Garfield permanently. Twenty-five beds arrived from different parts of the country so that the president would rest comfortably.

Several gifts were more unusual. A New York City woman sent Garfield white mice she thought would amuse him. The mice came with instructions to feed them bread and milk. Another woman forwarded a stuffed

hummingbird as decoration for the sickroom. One man mailed an eagle feather, suggesting that Garfield make a pen from it to sign his first official document after he recovered. This well-wisher also included a red garnet stone that Lucretia could set in a piece of jewelry.

According to newspaper reports, the president was facing his injury with courage and cheerfulness. A common theme in the press was that the nation—once divided by war—was now unified in hoping that Garfield recovered. "The whole country seemed to watch at his bedside," said one weekly magazine. "The heart of a great people beat with a single pulse, and a nation awoke at morning with the fervent hope that the President still lived."

It appeared to be true. The White House received thousands of letters and telegrams from every part of the nation. Individuals wrote that their families were praying for Garfield's recovery. Sunday school classes sent scripture passages. School groups and veterans organizations expressed their sympathy. Lucretia and others read these messages to the president to lift his spirits.

THE FAMILY COPES

After the doctors warned that Garfield's recuperation could be slow, the family decided that the two youngest children should remain in Ohio with relatives throughout the summer. Hal, Jim, and Mollie would stay in Washington until their father was able to travel to Mentor.

GARFIELD.

The Cloud of Sorrow and Humiliation Lifting from the Land.

Surgeon Bliss Now Willing to Be Quoted as Being Sure of a Recovery.

The Wound Healing from the Inside—A Deeper Drain-Pipe Used.

Yesterday's Maximum Figures: Pulse, 98; Temperature, 101; Respiration, 23.

Arrival of Conkling at Washington—A Visit of Condolence to Mrs. Garfield.

Confession of the Assasin, as Abridged by the District-Attorney.

A Recital That Will Curdle the Blood of All Christendom.

The Infamous Project Undertaken on the 18th of May, and Followed Without Intermission.

The Day Legally Set Apart to Fasting and Prayer in Kentucky and Arkansas.

LOWER FEVER.
8:30 A. M.

By mid-July, James Garfield seemed to be recovering from his injury. This column of headlines appeared in the *Chicago Daily Tribune*, July 15, 1881.

The three teens initially feared that Papa would die. But as the weeks of July passed, they felt optimistic. They treasured the rare times when they were allowed to visit him.

Lucretia encouraged her children to keep up their summer activities—seeing friends, going to the park, riding horses, and taking swimming lessons. They played billiards in the White House on the table their father had used. Jim and his friend watched the cooling machine being set up. Along with her mother, brothers, and family friends, Mollie went on carriage excursions around the city and took a boat to Mount Vernon, George Washington's former home, for a picnic.

Hal and Jim met with a tutor in the mornings as they prepared for the beginning of classes at Williams College in September. They both helped Brown with the influx of messages, telegrams, and letters and with the outgoing medical bulletins. Hal took it upon himself to send telegrams containing the doctors' updates to relatives and friends in Ohio.

Americans felt sympathy and affection for the Garfield family. Newspapers printed articles about the children and Garfield's mother, Eliza. An illustrated version of Lucretia's image appeared in the press with descriptions of her as a "self-sacrificing wife" and admirable mother and friend.

Cyrus Field, the businessman who spearheaded the laying of the first telegraph cable under the Atlantic Ocean, had befriended the Garfields long before the shooting. To help the family, he established a fund for Lucretia to which the public was invited to donate.

It started out with large contributions from wealthy businessmen. But as the fund received more press attention, ordinary people gave amounts as small as a dollar. The money was intended to support the family if President Garfield died or was permanently incapacitated by his injury. Less than three weeks after the shooting, more than $150,000 had been raised. Today, that would equal nearly $4,000,000.

A CONFESSION

Meanwhile, Charles Guiteau sat in jail, guarded by police and soldiers. Hate mail addressed to him flooded the warden's office. One contained a drawing of a scaffold from which a man labeled "Guiteau" hangs. Buzzards fly above and jackals crouch below.

Another congratulated Guiteau, saying that he would be rewarded. It was signed, "Yours until death, when we will have a happy reunion, SATAN."

In mid-July, District Attorney Corkhill gave the press Guiteau's confession, in which he described planning the shooting, buying the gun, and following the president around Washington. The confession changed the opinion of Americans who had previously withheld judgment. Guiteau didn't sound insane. He had prepared for the assassination too carefully and shown too much patience to be crazy.

Almon Rockwell read Garfield this account of the assassination attempt. The president listened without comment.

Corkhill received regular reports from the White House about Garfield's condition. On July 17, the president's four doctors informed Corkhill that, though they anticipated full recovery, they couldn't absolutely rule out death. In light of that opinion, the district attorney announced that he would wait until the president's situation was certain before moving forward with his case against Guiteau.

Corkhill ordered the jail warden to put Guiteau in a cell away from other

FRANK LESLIE'S
ILLUSTRATED

NEWSPAPER

Entered according to Act of Congress, in the year 1881, by Mrs. Frank Leslie, in the Office of the Librarian of Congress at Washington.—Entered at the Post Office, New York, N.Y., as Second-class Matter.

No. 1,347.—Vol. LII.   NEW YORK, JULY 23, 1881.   [Price 10 Cents. $4.00 Yearly. 13 Weeks, $1.00.

THE ATTEMPTED ASSASSINATION OF THE PRESIDENT.—A MORNING GREETING BY THE PRESIDENT'S WIFE AND DAUGHTER.
From a Sketch by a Staff Artist.—See Page 346.

prisoners and to forbid him from talking with the guards. Guiteau was not to have visitors nor receive or send mail unless it was preapproved by Corkhill.

Despite the news blackout, Guiteau gleaned information about the president's medical progress from the guards. He remained confident that he had the support and admiration of people throughout the nation. Surely, Arthur and the Stalwarts would protect him if Garfield died.

THE CRASH

Hope returned to the White House as Garfield seemed to gradually recover. On the evening of July 16, two weeks after his injury, the medical bulletin stated, "The President has passed a better day than any since he was shot." Four days later, the doctors reported that "the progress of the President toward recovery continues uninterruptedly." Lucretia told Harriet Blaine that "she considered him out of danger."

This news was a relief to an anxious public. The *Washington Post* proclaimed that, according to the president's doctors, he would be out of bed in two weeks.

On July 21, the day after the doctors' positive bulletin, they discovered cotton and wool fibers mixed with the pus coming from the wound. The bullet had driven pieces of Garfield's clothing into his body when he was shot. The following day, when doctors dressed the wound, they found a tiny piece of rib bone and more fibers discharged with the pus. As long as the wound kept draining well, though, they weren't worried.

On the night of July 22, everything suddenly changed. By morning, Garfield ran a high fever. He was sweating and having intense chills. His heart raced. He vomited several times. The president was in trouble.

Bliss sent for the expert surgeons, Agnew and Hamilton. The men immediately boarded a special train to Washington.

The front cover of *Frank Leslie's Illustrated Newspaper* contains an illustration of Garfield with Lucretia and Mollie by his bedside during mid-July.

JOSEPH LISTER'S WAR ON INFECTION

Joseph Lister (1827–1912)

Instead, the surgeons believed that infections came from foul air, called miasma, which contained poisons given off by rotting plant or animal material. To neutralize the poisons, military hospitals sprayed the chemicals in the air and on smelly body waste.

By the end of the war, scientists in Europe uncovered evidence that it was germs, not poisonous miasma, that attacked the body. In France, chemist Louis Pasteur (1822–1895) proved that microbes caused plant and animal material to decay. His experiments showed that these germs could be killed by heat or particular chemicals. Still, his discovery wasn't widely accepted.

ACID TEST

Joseph Lister, a surgeon in Scotland, was impressed by Pasteur's work. Lister worried about the high number of hospital patients who died after undergoing surgeries such as leg amputations or repair of deep knife gashes. In 1865, he tested Pasteur's research on his patients.

Unlike Civil War surgeons who used antiseptic chemicals *after* a wound became infected, Lister's goal was to kill microbes in wounds *before* they caused an infection. He tried various chemicals and ways of applying them to wounds. Lister concluded that carbolic acid was the best at preventing infection. In spring 1867, he published his study in a respected British medical journal. He explained that when he washed open wounds with carbolic acid, fewer patients died.

Lister emphasized that pus was *not* a sign of healing. It was a sign of bacterial infection. Microbes, not miasma, caused an infection.

During the Civil War (1861–1865), military surgeons—including Garfield's doctors—observed that certain wound infections spread from patient to patient in a hospital. They found that if they cleaned an infected wound with chemicals such as carbolic acid, bromine, nitric acid, and iodine, they could sometimes heal it.

These antiseptic measures worked because the chemicals killed bacteria. But Civil War doctors didn't know that infection-causing bacteria even existed.

When germs were kept away from wounds, he wrote, pus didn't form.

Lister recommended that doctors put a diluted carbolic acid solution on wounds after injury or surgery and also soak bandages and dressings in the chemical. He suspected that bacteria entered wounds through a surgeon's dirty hands and instruments. For that reason, he urged doctors to wash their hands thoroughly and to sterilize hands and surgical instruments with carbolic acid. Lister developed a device to spray the acid solution in the air around an open wound when surgeons operated and changed dressings.

Some British physicians praised his antiseptic methods as an effective way to stop infection. Other doctors claimed that Lister's method made no difference in wound healing.

But after military surgeons in France and Germany used the methods successfully during the Franco-Prussian War of 1870, Lister's approach gained acceptance in Europe. Eventually, most of the British medical community adopted his antiseptic advice, too.

AMERICAN DOUBTERS

The majority of American surgeons remained doubtful. In 1876, five years before Garfield was

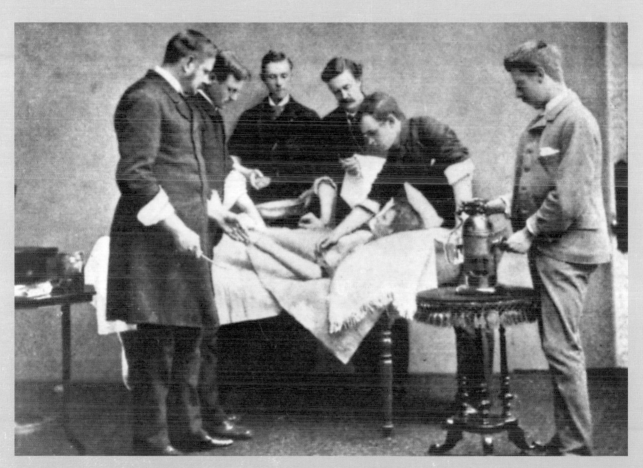

This photograph, taken between 1870 and 1880, shows Scottish surgeons using Lister's antiseptic method. A sprayer produced a fine yellow mist of carbolic acid around the surgical site. Instruments and hands passed through the spray, presumably being disinfected, as the doctors worked on the patient. At this time, surgeons did not wear gowns, caps, or gloves to prevent microbes from entering the open wound.

121

shot, Joseph Lister sailed across the Atlantic Ocean to the United States to make his case. Trying to persuade the Americans of the value of antiseptic methods, he gave lectures about germs, pus, and infection. Lister also demonstrated surgeries using carbolic acid.

Many American doctors, including Garfield's, still refused to accept that microbes caused infection. Dr. D. W. Bliss was one who thought that germ theory was unproven. Others didn't see why Lister's efforts were worth the time and bother. Dr. Frank Hamilton considered the methods to be useful only after pus and blood oozed from a wound. He said the procedures were unnecessary and too complicated to follow before surgery and in preparing dressings.

Dr. D. Hayes Agnew, however, didn't dismiss Lister's ideas. In Agnew's opinion, even if the controversial germ theory did not explain the development of pus, his patients benefited from antiseptic methods. In his 1878 textbook on surgery, Agnew recommended many of the procedures and included a drawing of Lister's carbolic acid sprayer. Joseph Lister changed other minds, too, particularly those of America's younger doctors.

Yet even surgeons who believed they were following Lister's guidelines were still exposing patients to germs. Doctors often skipped the step of scrupulously washing their hands and fingernails with soap and water before treating a wound or performing surgery.

In other cases, doctors didn't adequately disinfect their instruments or hands in carbolic acid, or they used a solution too weak to kill bacteria. If they dropped an instrument on the floor, they picked it up and inserted it into a patient's body without cleaning it again. Surgeons continued the common habit of holding a knife between their teeth to free their hands while operating.

On the day of Garfield's shooting, Drs. Townshend, Bliss, and Wales probed the president's bullet wound with unwashed fingers and unsterilized metal instruments. Neither the wound nor the dressing put on it were cleaned and disinfected until more than seven hours after the shooting. Lister warned that these practices allowed bacteria to enter the body and cause infection.

Dr. Robert Reyburn claimed that he and the president's other doctors followed Lister's antiseptic advice when changing dressings. He said that the instruments, tubing, and solutions used to wash out Garfield's wound each day were disinfected as Lister recommended. Eleven years

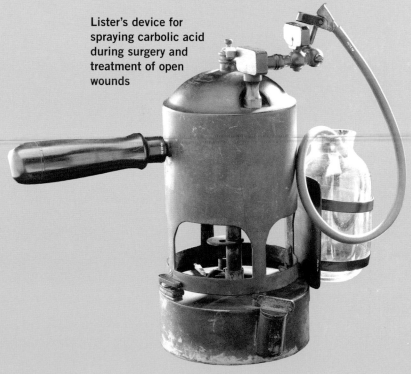

Lister's device for spraying carbolic acid during surgery and treatment of open wounds

later, however, he admitted that the method of surgical care "was not so thoroughly appreciated or carried out by operating surgeons in 1881 as it is in 1892."

The constant probing of the president's wound, insertions of tubes, and surgical incisions created plenty of opportunities for bacteria to enter Garfield's body.

By the end of the nineteenth century, the American medical community finally accepted the principles of germ theory. Further discoveries by Pasteur, German scientist Robert Koch (1843–1910), and others provided solid evidence that microbes caused disease and infection.

As more effective procedures were developed, surgery and wound treatment became safer. After scientists tested disinfecting methods, they found that carbolic acid wasn't the best way to kill germs, especially in the concentrations generally used. Heat—dry or from hot water—sterilized surgical instruments much better. Researchers also learned that the primary source of wound infection was not air, but contact with hands, instruments, and even drops from a surgeon's mouth and nose. By 1887, Lister gave up the use of his carbolic sprayer, and by the late-1890s, surgeons began to wear masks.

These advancements came too late for James Garfield.

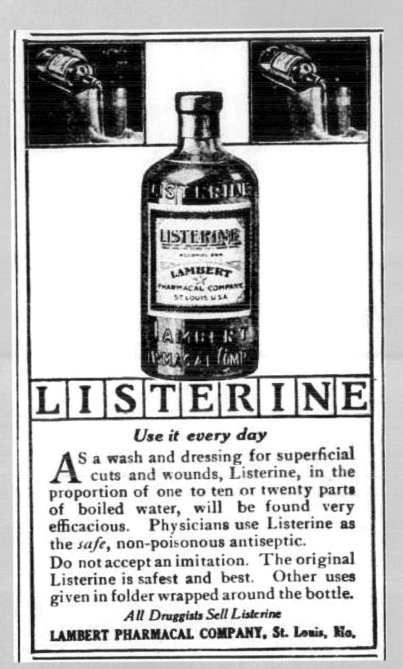

One convert to Lister's ideas was Dr. Joseph Joshua Lawrence. In 1879, he mixed a chemical similar to carbolic acid with alcohol and flavorings to create a product later marketed as Listerine. The liquid was promoted as an antiseptic to treat cuts and wounds and to cure colds, sore throats, diarrhea, skin diseases, mouth sores, and other ailments. This Listerine advertisement appeared in a 1914 newspaper.

VOL. IX.–No. 230. AUGUST 3, 1881. Price, 10 Cents.

PUBLISHED BY
KEPPLER & SCHWARZMANN.

NEW YORK
TRADE MARK REGISTERED 1878

OFFICE No. 21 – 23 WARREN ST.

"ENTERED AT THE POST OFFICE AT NEW YORK, AND ADMITTED FOR TRANSMISSION THROUGH THE MAILS AT SECOND CLASS RATES"

CHAPTER ELEVEN

THE CHANNEL OF PUS

> "You must keep up courage & never let it fail."
>
> —Willie Reinig, age fifteen, Des Moines, Iowa

WHEN AGNEW AND HAMILTON ENTERED THE SICKROOM ON Sunday morning, July 24, they were alarmed to find the president covered with sweat. The other doctors said that he had been perspiring profusely throughout the night. They all recognized the symptoms. A severe infection had overtaken Garfield's body.

As the two surgeons examined him, they found a sac full of pus under his skin three inches below the bullet hole. They'd have to open it so that the pus could drain out.

Bliss gave the president the news, warning him that it would be a painful procedure.

"Very well," Garfield said, without hesitating. "Whatever you say is necessary must be done."

Agnew did the cutting, with Hamilton assisting. They sprayed Garfield's skin with ether, but it wasn't enough to completely dull the pain. Without crying out or flinching, Garfield endured the slice of the scalpel as Agnew made a two-and-a-half-inch incision. He cut down

This cover from *Puck* magazine shows malaria swirling around the White House as the president lay inside suffering from his wound. A New York company sent a pamphlet to the White House promoting its American Ozone Generator, which was guaranteed to purify the air of the disease. In 1881, no one knew that the way to eliminate malaria was to prevent infected mosquitoes from breeding and biting.

into Garfield's flesh more than an inch to open up an exit for the pus. Then the surgeons inserted a rubber drainage tube.

The pus flowed out, but not well enough. Within two days, Garfield redeveloped the same symptoms: high fever, profuse sweating, chills, vomiting. Agnew operated again to enlarge the opening. He removed small pieces of bone from the wound, likely splintered off the rib when the bullet slammed into Garfield's body. Agnew inserted two rubber tubes to drain the pus filling the channel that extended down from the bullet wound.

WHERE'S THE BULLET?

Initially, the surgeons hadn't wanted to operate on Garfield to search for the bullet. The risks of cutting into the abdomen or chest were great, and he appeared to be recovering. If his body had harmlessly formed a cyst around the bullet, there was no reason to take the chance.

As Garfield's progress slowed, and especially after his distressing relapse, the doctors began to consider removing the bullet in order to save his life. But precisely where was it? They hadn't found it with their probes. Was there a way to pinpoint its location so that they could make an incision directly above that spot?

The public offered solutions for dealing with the bullet. One idea involved turning the president upside down for several hours and allowing gravity to pull the bullet toward the entry hole, where it could be easily lifted out. Another suggestion was to attach one end of a rubber tube to an air pump while sticking the other end into the wound until it reached the bullet. By turning on the pump, the bullet could be sucked out.

A New York medical school professor performed an experiment to track the bullet's probable path. Using a gun like Guiteau's, he shot into human cadavers that were about the size of James Garfield. Then he dissected the bodies. The professor concluded that Guiteau's bullet likely hit Garfield's rib and was

A HINT FOR THE DISPOSAL OF GUITEAU.

LET A CONSULTATION BE HELD ON HIM.

deflected downward into the pelvic region, where it remained. In the professor's opinion, the bullet rested against important nerves, and he recommended leaving it there. He shared his experimental results with Dr. Hamilton.

After probing the pus channel, Hamilton and the medical team had come to almost the same conclusion. They were convinced that the bullet lay somewhere in the muscles of the lower abdomen near the groin.

A young Washington doctor had a different idea about the bullet's location. Basing his hypothesis on newspaper reports of Garfield's symptoms, Dr. Frank Baker drew a diagram two days after the shooting to show where he thought the bullet penetrated. He guessed that it had traveled

A cartoon from August 10, 1881, comments on the many doctors attempting to heal Garfield. It suggests that to punish Guiteau, he should be subjected to the same treatment of elixirs, pills, and probing that Garfield was enduring.

to the left after entering Garfield's back and was somewhere on that side of his body.

Baker showed his drawing to a few colleagues, including two of the doctors who attended Garfield at the train station. But Baker didn't speak to Bliss or to any of Garfield's new physicians, especially after they stated that the bullet had gone down the right side toward the pelvis. Baker decided it would be professionally improper to push his opposing view when he hadn't examined the wound.

BELL CALLING

Garfield's medical team heard of another way to locate the bullet. They considered it promising primarily because of the man who proposed it. Alexander Graham Bell, famous for inventing the telephone five years earlier, suggested using induction balance, with which he had worked while perfecting his invention.

The induction-balance apparatus used coils of electricity-conducting wire to detect metal. Bell thought he could modify the device to find the bullet in Garfield's body. The procedure would be done externally, and the president wouldn't feel it.

On July 14, the doctors invited Bell to the White House. He took a basket of grapes and a sympathy note to Lucretia, which he handed to Brown before going in to speak with Bliss and Woodward. After hearing the details, the doctors encouraged Bell to develop the equipment for use on the president.

He and his colleague Charles Sumner Tainter went to work in Bell's Washington laboratory, using their own ideas and input from other scientists whom they had contacted by letter and telegram. The two men constructed an instrument that included batteries, coils of wire to carry electric current, and a telephone receiver. When the coils passed over a metal object, the telephone transmitted a sound similar to a musical tone.

Twelve days later, on the evening of July 26, the men were ready to try the device on Garfield. Bell and Tainter entered the sickroom and greeted the president. Bell was stunned by his appearance. "His face is very pale—or rather it is of an ashen grey colour which makes one feel for a moment that you are not looking upon a living man," he wrote his wife. "It made my heart bleed to look at him and think of all he must have suffered to bring him to this."

No wonder. That morning, Dr. Agnew had enlarged the incision on Garfield's back, taken out pieces of bone, and inserted two drainage tubes.

Garfield lay on his left side. His head rested on the shoulder of one of his attendants, and his arms held on to the man's neck. The bed covers and clothing were pulled aside to expose the president's back, including the dressings over his bullet wound and new incision.

Bell planned for Tainter to control the device's electric coils. Instead, Bliss took over. The doctor held the detector over Garfield's back, moving it downward from the wound along the spine. Bell was surprised. From what he'd been told, the doctors believed the bullet was in the president's front abdomen.

The room was quiet. Nobody spoke.

Bell held the telephone receiver to his ear, listening for the same sound he'd heard in his tests when the device detected a metal bullet. But the equipment wasn't operating as he expected. Bell knew the results weren't reliable.

BACK TO THE LAB

Returning to their laboratory, Bell and Tainter adjusted the instrument. Then they visited the Soldiers' Home in Washington, a retirement home for old and disabled veterans. The men tested the metal detector on three former Civil War soldiers who each had a bullet in a known location of the body. The machine failed to work unless the bullet was close to the skin surface. Still, the experiment helped Bell and Tainter figure out how to make modifications.

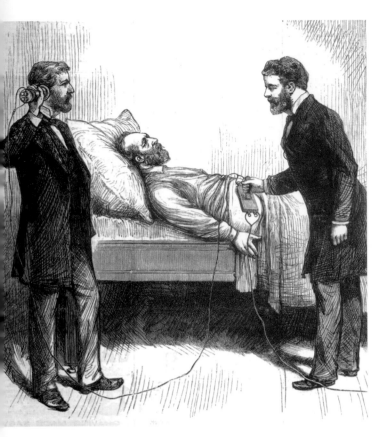

An illustration in *Harper's Weekly*, August 13, 1881, shows Alexander Graham Bell and Charles Sumner Tainter using the induction balance equipment to find the bullet in President Garfield's body. The bullet was actually on the left side of his body, not where they held the device.

A few days later, they retested the device on one of the soldiers. This time it accurately located the bullet in the man's back. In further tests, Bell and Tainter were able to detect a lead bullet up to five inches away from the coils.

Confident that they'd fixed the initial problems, Bell sent word to Dr. Bliss. On August 1, he and Tainter returned to the White House.

Standing next to the president's bed, Tainter moved the detector above the right side of Garfield's abdomen, where his doctors believed the bullet had ended up. Bell listened for the telltale tone on the telephone receiver. He heard a pulsating sound, yet it was different from previous successful tests.

Bliss and the other doctors believed this sound proved that the bullet was in the lower right front of the abdomen, just as they suspected. They reported the news to the press.

Bell knew better. Something had gone wrong with the test. He hadn't pinpointed the bullet with enough accuracy for the surgeons to remove it.

The next day he visited the White House in search of an explanation. He found out that the president rested on two mattresses, and the bottom one contained steel wire springs. Although the metal might have interfered with his apparatus, Bell decided that the effect wasn't enough to explain the results from the day before. The problem had to be his device.

He and Tainter continued to tinker. The inventors hoped that if they improved their device, it would be a valuable tool for all surgeons. After more

ALEXANDER GRAHAM BELL

Born in Scotland and educated in London, England, Bell moved to Canada with his parents when he was twenty-three. Using techniques he learned from his father, Bell began to teach the deaf, helping his students speak and read lips. He later moved to Boston, where he opened a school.

Inspired by his interest in hearing, sound, and speech, Bell experimented with using electricity to transmit voices. In 1876, he

Bell with his wife, Mabel, and two daughters, in 1885. Mabel became deaf at age four and, as a teen, was one of Bell's Boston students before they married.

Alexander Graham Bell (1847–1922), age thirty-five, in a portrait painted a year after he tried to find the bullet in President Garfield's body

received a patent for his telephone. The next year, he became a founder of the Bell Telephone Company, which evolved into the American Telephone and Telegraph Company (AT&T).

Throughout his life, Bell created many other inventions, including those that paved the way for the development of airplanes and phonograph records.

He and his wife, Mabel, had two daughters who lived into their eighties and two sons who died as infants. One of those sons, Edward, passed away in August 1881 during the time Bell was working on the bullet-detecting device in Washington.

weeks of trial and error and testing and retesting, they succeeded in locating a bullet lost in a different man's body for years. But their success didn't come in time to help Garfield.

FALSE HOPE

The news of the president's late-July relapse shocked and disappointed everyone, including his doctors. When he temporarily bounced back after the July surgeries, there was hope that Garfield was on the path to recovery again. It didn't last.

Although newspaper headlines and articles were optimistic, the public wasn't getting the whole story. Reyburn later revealed that Bliss insisted on upbeat medical bulletins—even if they misrepresented the president's health. Bliss argued that Garfield would see the reports in the newspapers, and any

The daily medical updates from Garfield's physicians led the public to believe he was on the mend. On August 4, a fireworks display in Brooklyn celebrated his recovery. From *Frank Leslie's Illustrated Newspaper*, August 20, 1881.

negative information would discourage him and affect his recuperation.

Reyburn and the rest of Garfield's medical team felt uncomfortable lying to the nation. "These bulletins were often the subject of animated and sometimes heated discussion between Dr. Bliss and the other attending surgeons," Reyburn wrote, "the surgeons usually taking one side of the question and Dr. Bliss the other."

The White House staff was careful to hide the president's true condition, too. Even as Garfield's health worsened, Brown sent out telegrams saying: "Rumors concerning unfavorable change in Presidents condition largely sensational," and "Surgeons believe President is prospectively better than at any time since shooting."

Harriet Blaine had a more accurate view of the situation from her visits to the White House during which she talked to people who saw the president. She wrote her children on July 31, "Plainly I do not see how he is to recover." Three weeks later, Harriet heard news from one of the other cabinet wives: Dr. Edson was admitting that she had lost hope.

Lucretia spent most of every day at her husband's bedside. Even if she feared the worst, she stayed positive, lifting his spirits when they sagged.

After the shooting, James Garfield had little direct contact with anyone except his White House caregivers. On August 11, however, he wrote this letter to his mother in Hiram, Ohio: "Don't be disturbed by conflicting reports about my condition. It is true I am still weak, and on my back, but I am gaining every day, and need only time and patience to bring me through. Give my love to all the relatives & friends & especially to sisters Hitty and Mary. Your loving son —James A. Garfield." He was hiding the truth from her. By then, Garfield had already undergone surgeries to deal with the raging infection in his body.

Garfield's children remained in the dark about their father's condition. Mollie wrote in her diary on August 1, "Papa doing gloriously; improving all the time."

Hal continued sending reassuring telegrams to their family in Ohio.

On August 4, shortly before his father was to face another surgery to release rapidly accumulating pus, Jim wrote, "Papa doing splendidly."

CRISIS

As his infection intensified, Garfield heavily perspired and ran a high fever. Cleaning out the wound channel hadn't stopped the body's relentless release of pus. It was building up faster than it could drain out.

On August 8, Dr. Agnew again performed surgery to open another exit for the pus. This time, Reyburn administered ether, which Garfield inhaled so that he would sleep during the procedure.

The surgery didn't help. The bacteria kept multiplying, and the pus kept flowing. Eventually, the doctors could extend a flexible probe twelve inches from the bullet hole down the pus channel. Although the medical team didn't realize it, rinsing out the channel two or three times a day did no good. The carbolic acid

ON THE BRINK

Of the River of Death

Another Critical Period

For President Garfield

His Condition Very Alarming

Leaving Little Hope of Recovery

Intense Excitement in Washington

And Throughout the Country

Slight Improvement in Evening

Maintained at Latest Reports.

Surgeons Anxious But Hopeful

Incidents of an Anxious Day.

Headlines from the *St. Paul [MN] Daily Globe* on August 17, 1881, report on Garfield's grave condition. The article reported that the mood in the White House is "a general feeling of anxiety and actual alarm."

solution was too weak to kill bacteria, and the procedure only introduced more microbes.

Garfield was failing. Every dressing change was agonizing. He couldn't keep food down. Yet Bliss tried to push hard-to-digest foods on him, such as steak, lamb chops, and beef. The president was constantly given morphine, quinine, whiskey, and brandy, which likely irritated his already sensitive digestive system.

In the six weeks since the shooting, Garfield had lost nearly 80 pounds and changed from a robust and slightly overweight man weighing 210 pounds to a skeletal figure. It was not the look of a man in recovery.

The doctors resorted to giving him nourishment with enemas several times a day. The method involved injecting a solution of beef broth, milk, whiskey, egg yolks, and opium into his rectum. The procedure wasn't effective because the rectum and large intestine absorbed few nutrients from the mixture, not enough to sustain a man. Garfield was starving to death.

In mid August, both Secretary of War Robert Todd Lincoln and Silas Boynton confided to friends that Garfield was definitely in critical condition. On the same day, Bliss told reporters that "the wound looks better than at any time yet," and the official bulletin described the president as "somewhat restless" and "tranquil."

POISON PUS

The river of pus continued to ooze out the drainage tubes. Bliss discovered that the pus wasn't as healthy as he once insisted. While dressing the president's wound, he accidentally cut himself. Bliss's infected finger became so swollen and sore that he had to keep his arm in a sling.

Soon new problems arose. A salivary gland in front of Garfield's right ear swelled. The pain was excruciating, and his face was partially paralyzed. The doctors shaved off his whiskers so that they could cut into the gland and free the pus. They used no anesthetic.

But the gland didn't heal. A combination of pus and saliva leaked from the gland back into Garfield's mouth and ear canal. He could only take in small amounts of cracked ice and water through his mouth.

Abscesses the size of peas appeared in his armpits and on his chest and back. The doctors cut them open, letting their bacteria-laden contents flow out of Garfield's body. Fluid started to accumulate in his lungs.

The bad news could no longer be hidden. By the end of August, the hope of the nation began to turn into the dreadful realization that Garfield might not recover. After closely following his day-to-day progress for nearly two months, people viewed him differently than they had previous presidents.

Garfield's doctors released this medical bulletin on August 22, 1881. In it, they report that he "has not vomited" since the day before and "his general condition is more encouraging than when the last bulletin was issued." But instead of gradually recovering, Garfield was getting worse every day.

"Party difference has disappeared in universal admiration of his tranquil heroism," the editors of *Harper's Weekly* wrote, "and there is probably a more general affection and confidence felt for General Garfield than for any President since Washington."

Garfield's medical care appalled doctors who trusted Joseph Lister's antiseptic methods. They believed that probing the wound was more harmful than the bullet itself. If the instruments and drainage tubes were not properly disinfected, they would carry dangerous bacteria deep into the body. Garfield's abscesses and worsening condition were signs that poor treatment had led to blood poisoning.

Bliss denied this and chastised those who offered an opinion even though they weren't on the case. Hamilton pushed back, too, telling a reporter at the end of August, "I consider that his chances of recovery are better at present than they have ever been since he received the injury."

Garfield's medical team received some support from the press. Articles accused their detractors of basing comments on brief medical bulletins and newspaper reports, hardly enough to make a diagnosis. The critics were jealous, the articles said, and looking for ways to besmirch the respected surgeons involved in Garfield's care. The wound was so serious that only doctors with skill and dedication, like Garfield's, could have kept him alive and put him on the road to recovery.

Meanwhile, the president grew weaker. His immune system couldn't fight the bacteria spreading through his bloodstream and ravaging his body.

ESCAPE

Garfield understood the gravity of his condition. Weary and weak, he felt pain from the infected wound and the doctors' treatment of it. Yet through it all, he didn't complain. Edson later said, "I never heard a groan from him during his whole sickness." Her remark was echoed by others who cared for him.

Beginning in late-July, Garfield made comments to those closest to him (Lucretia, Boynton, Edson, Rockwell, and Swaim), hinting that he knew he was probably dying from his wound. And at the end of August, when churches throughout the country held a day of prayer for him, Reyburn told Garfield about the many people praying for him. The president responded glumly, "I am glad of it; I have need of them."

Perhaps sensing the hopelessness of his situation, Garfield yearned to leave the cramped, depressing White House sickroom and the foul smell of Washington's swamps that wafted in through the open windows. He ached to be outside, to see the sky, to gaze at the sea.

Bliss put him off, but Garfield was insistent. "I want to get away," he told the doctor firmly.

Finally deciding the change might do him good, the medical team and the president's aides investigated how they could grant his wish.

A rich businessman, Charles Francklyn, offered his twenty-room summer home by the Atlantic Ocean in Elberon, New Jersey. Lucretia had responded well to the sea air while she recovered from malaria at the Elberon Hotel, and Garfield had enjoyed his week in June there.

The arrangements were made. Sixty-six days after he fell wounded onto the floor of the Baltimore and Potomac station, James Garfield would leave Washington.

CHAPTER TWELVE
ELBERON

"I have always felt that the ocean was my friend,
and the sight of it brings rest and peace."

—President James Garfield, diary entry two weeks before the shooting

LUCRETIA WAS WORRIED ABOUT THE RISKS OF MOVING HER HUSBAND. Garfield would have to be carried out of the White House, transported to the train, and moved to a bed at the New Jersey cottage. The trip to Elberon would last about seven hours. Once he was taken from the air-cooled sickroom, the hot weather might sap the little energy he had left.

Could he withstand the strain on his weakening body? Lucretia prayed that he could and that the decision to go to the sea was the right one.

Harriet Blaine wrote her daughter of the dilemma: "Poor dear Gaffy, how wretched it is! Wounded and sore and hurt to the death, he now to save his life, must dare to lose it."

DELICATE TRANSPORT

When Dr. Bliss entered the sickroom early on Monday morning, September 5, Garfield greeted him impatiently. "Well, is this the last day in the White House?"

An illustration appearing in *Harper's Weekly* shows President Garfield being removed from the White House on the morning of September 6, 1881. Lucretia and Mollie stand on the left.

Hal and Jim had left for Williams College on a train the night before after saying goodbye to their father. The farewell was difficult for them. Jim wrote in his diary, "I do not care to go."

Bliss attempted to tamp down the president's excitement, afraid that it would raise his temperature and heart rate.

Garfield was tired of being calmed down. "No, no," he told the doctor, "I don't want any more delay."

And there wasn't. Everything had been organized and, by 6:00 a.m. the next day, the mission had begun.

By lifting Garfield's bedsheet as he lay upon it, a group of doctors and attendants gently shifted him from his bed onto a stretcher. The stretcher had been designed to be carried down the White House stairs while keeping the patient horizontal.

Meanwhile, other men took Garfield's mattress downstairs. At the bottom of the staircase, Garfield was moved onto it and carried outside.

Waiting by the White House entrance was a large, heavy wagon equipped with a platform and bed springs to absorb the jolts as the wagon drove to the train station. Garfield and his mattress were carefully loaded onto the wagon. A few of his doctors and attendants climbed in beside him.

The night before had been stiflingly hot, and the early morning was already steaming and miserable. A wet cloth on the president's forehead cooled him off. Rockwell fanned him.

As the wagon pulled away, Garfield waved to his White House staff gathered on the porch. Outside the gate, a crowd of nearly one hundred fifty waited to bid him goodbye. The people followed the wagon as it headed several blocks to the train station.

The police had cleared the street of other wagons and carriages. Despite the early hour, hundreds more well-wishers joined the procession behind the president or stood along the sidewalk silently paying tribute to him.

Railroad workers had laid a temporary track between the main line and the street so that the wagon could pull up next to the president's rail car. Police officers strung ropes to keep back the crowd who came to the area to see Garfield off.

Strong men lifted Garfield and the mattress from the wagon onto the rail car, which had been retrofitted to accommodate him. He was transferred onto a specially designed thick mattress nestled atop a box full of cushions. To minimize the president's pain as the train rocked and bumped along the tracks, this box was raised off the floor by boards supported by more cushions.

Wire screens on the outside of the windows kept dust from entering the car during the journey. Heavy curtains and thick carpet muffled the sounds from the train wheels. Ice placed around the inside of the car kept it cooler.

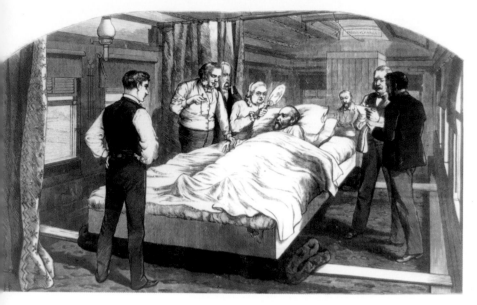

The interior of the railcar that took President Garfield to the New Jersey seaside. A cushion of mattresses reduced the jolting and vibration as the train traveled as fast as sixty miles an hour. Dr. Bliss takes Garfield's pulse, and Dr. Edson fans him. Illustration from *Leslie's Illustrated Newspaper*, September 24, 1881

The doctors rode with Garfield. For the first part of the trip, Lucretia remained by her husband's side, fanning him. After that, she moved back and forth from the adjacent car where Mollie and the rest of the president's friends, attendants, and aides sat. A third car held twenty soldiers to lift the president and his mattress in Elberon, and the fourth was for baggage.

Cabinet members and their wives were scheduled to follow on the regularly scheduled train to New Jersey later that morning.

At 6:30 a.m., the president's special train departed the city where he had been shot, carrying him to the sea and—everyone hoped—recovery.

The railroad made an additional change to ensure a comfortable journey. To avoid the usual loud noises and whistles of approaching trains, officials notified trains coming south on adjacent tracks to stop as the president neared.

When Garfield's train passed stations along the way, local people waved American flags and stood with their hats off in respect.

TO THE SEA

Throughout the country, towns and cities proclaimed Tuesday, September 6, as a day of prayer. While the train traveled toward New Jersey, worshippers attended church services to pray for Garfield's recovery. Government offices in Washington and other cities, as well as many stores, closed for the day. In some places, school was dismissed.

Crowds gathered around news bulletin boards to read how Garfield was tolerating the trip. Yet no reporters accompanied the president. To keep the public informed, Brown arranged a solution with reporters. He wrote out the regular medical bulletins. As the train slowed down at each railroad station, Brown tossed the latest update out the window to an Associated Press agent, who spread the news by telegraph.

This 1885 photograph shows Francklyn Cottage on the right and the Elberon Hotel on the left. Although Charles Francklyn's summer home was called a cottage, it was a twenty-room mansion. The Garfields had stayed at the hotel during their June vacation while Lucretia was recovering from malaria.

In Elberon the night before, under nearly a full moon, hundreds of railroad workers had toiled in the oppressive heat. The usual quiet in the beach town was broken by the sound of sledgehammers driving metal spikes into wooden ties as the men laid more than a half-mile of track from the station to Francklyn Cottage. The new spur enabled Garfield's train to move up to the cottage's porch, sparing him a wagon ride over rough roads.

After twenty-four hours of hard work, the men finished the track in time for the president's arrival. Shortly after 1:00 that afternoon, the train appeared.

Unfortunately, the engine didn't have the power to get the cars up the incline to the cottage. To solve the problem, rail workers and strong bystanders unhooked the cars from the engine and pushed them the last few hundred yards to the side porch. Garfield was lifted out and carried inside.

The final hour of the trip had taken a toll on him. His temperature increased, and he was exhausted. But by 10:30 that night, his fever dropped and he fell asleep.

Boynton told a reporter that his cousin was weak from the trip. "The President has been a very sick man for the past 10 days. In that time he has not gained in the least. You should remember that he has not had much reserve to draw upon."

Workmen laid temporary railroad track from the nearby train station to Francklyn Cottage. The job was finished in twenty-four hours as men worked through the night under light from lanterns and the moon. Townspeople and the Elberon Hotel provided food and lemonade. The illustration appeared in *Frank Leslie's Illustrated Newspaper*, September 24, 1881.

After the tracks were torn up, a private citizen bought the wooden railroad ties to build a small tea house not far from the cottage, painting it red, white, and blue. Today the tea house sits a few blocks from the former site of the Francklyn Cottage.

ROOM WITH A VIEW

Garfield's bed was set up in a large open room on the cottage's second floor, positioned so that he could look out the window. He was pleased to be able to see the ocean and hear the waves breaking. A refreshing breeze cooled the room, and he was comfortable.

Bliss announced that the president wanted to reduce the number of doctors around him. Whether Garfield actually said that is unclear. Within two days of arriving at Elberon, all the doctors returned to Washington except Bliss and the surgeons Agnew and Hamilton. Edson departed as well, worn out by the previous two months of providing care. Boynton remained to perform nursing duties.

By the time Reyburn left Garfield's side, along with the other Washington doctors, he felt that there was little he or anyone else could do. "It was perfectly apparent to all the attending surgeons," Reyburn wrote later, "that

A crowd watches as men push Garfield's rail car the final yards to the door of Francklyn Cottage. Armed guards patrol the perimeter of the property. From *Frank Leslie's Illustrated Newspaper*, September 24, 1881

the President's life could not be prolonged for more than a few days after the date of his trip to Elberon."

Harriet Blaine shared that opinion. After visiting the cottage with cabinet members and their wives, she wrote her children, "He is just the same. I do not believe he will recover."

Yet over the next several days, Bliss's bulletins were positive. The president was responding well to the sea air, they said. "His general condition appears more encouraging."

Bliss rarely allowed Garfield to meet with his cabinet, and then for only a few minutes. Secretary of War Lincoln visited eight days after Garfield arrived in Elberon. He hadn't seen the president since the shooting. Lincoln was shaken. Before him lay a weak, emaciated man who, nonetheless, cheerfully greeted him.

When Bliss finally permitted it, Garfield was lifted onto a reclining chair by the window so that he had a better view outside. The president felt as if "he was himself again" when he saw people swimming and walking at the beach, boats sailing on the ocean, and the soldiers pacing the perimeter of the cottage lawn. He told the doctors that he wished he'd been brought to Elberon weeks earlier.

Garfield stayed good-natured, sometimes showing his sense of humor. One day while Mollie fanned her papa, she fainted from the heat. Garfield called to Lucretia, using an expression common during his childhood in the Ohio woods, "Why, the child fell like a log!" Mollie quickly revived, and Lucretia enjoyed hearing her husband's wit again.

GUITEAU, A TARGET

While James Garfield struggled to recover in Elberon, Charles Guiteau remained confined to his Washington cell. Public threats against Guiteau had ramped up as Garfield's condition worsened during August. Authorities were determined to prevent a lynch mob from storming the District of Columbia jail. Besides the regular prison guards, a group of U.S. Army soldiers was assigned to it.

When the soldiers were changing shifts early on a rainy Sunday evening, September 11, one of them did what others had threatened. Sergeant John Mason strode to a spot where he could see Guiteau's cell window. After he spotted Guiteau looking out, Mason aimed his rifle and fired.

As his fellow soldiers reacted in disbelief, Mason handed over his weapon to the squad captain. "I intended to kill the scoundrel," he said calmly. "I did not enlist to guard an assassin." He had planned ahead to shoot Guiteau, and he didn't regret his action. Mason later told a reporter that Guiteau "had shot a good man, the President of this great Nation, and I thought it was my duty to kill him."

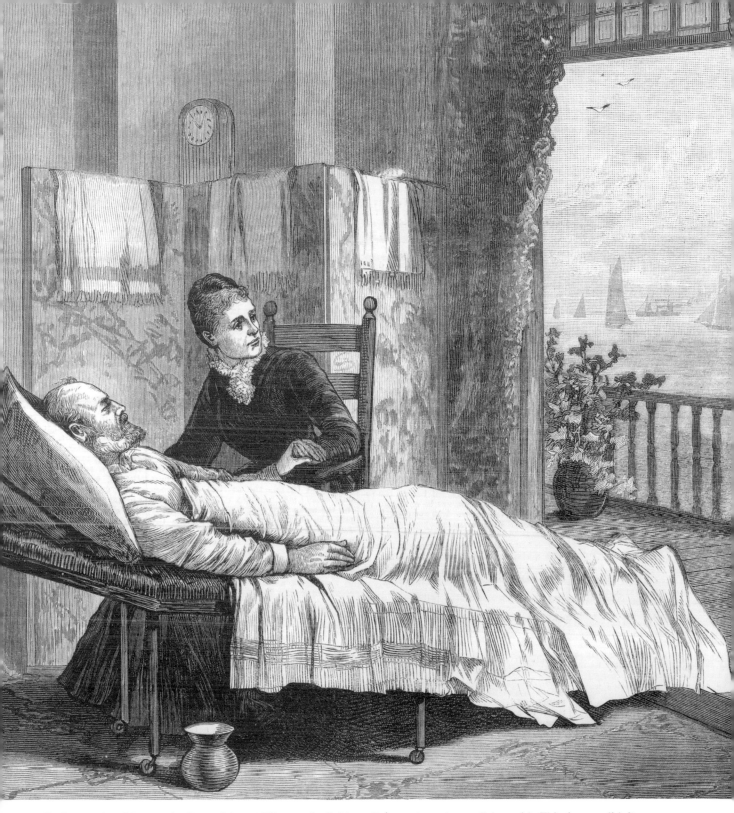

On September 13, a week after arriving at Elberon, Garfield lay on a reclining chair by his room's window. Lucretia sat by his side. He savored the experience. "This is delightful; it is such a change," he said. This image didn't appear until the October 1, 1881, issue of *Frank Leslie's Illustrated Newspaper*.

When the jail guards heard Guiteau cry out, they immediately unlocked his cell door. They found him cowering in the corner, loudly praying. Guiteau was terrified, but unhurt. The shot missed his body by just a few inches and struck the wall behind him.

Although Guiteau was unharmed, Sergeant Mason was arrested. He would later face an army court-martial. Some of Mason's fellow soldiers said they were sorry his aim had been off. When the public read about the incident, many shared the same regret and donated money to a fund for his defense.

A GRAVE SITUATION

Bliss continued to release medical bulletins that played down Garfield's failing health, going so far as to say on September 15, "He has certainly not retrograded, but, on the contrary, has made some progress toward convalescence."

Boynton told reporters that those bulletins were wrong. The virulent infection inside Garfield's body had spread.

Pus kept draining from the gunshot wound. Garfield developed pus-filled sores on his back, which the surgeons cut open. His lung infection worsened, and he coughed up pus and mucous in fits that exhausted him. He had periods of chills followed by sweating. At times, he hallucinated.

When Agnew heard Bliss imply that Garfield would be cured, he told a friend privately that he long believed the case was hopeless. "The President may live the day out," said Agnew, "and possibly to-morrow; but he cannot live a week."

Most everyone besides Bliss had accepted that the end was near. Cabinet members not already in Elberon were on their way.

Garfield seemed to know, too. From his bed, he called Agnew over. "Doctor, am I not critically ill?"

Unlike Bliss, Agnew believed in being straightforward. "Your condition is critical," he replied.

Garfield simply said, "I thought so."

The president began complaining of occasional chest pain. His body temperature dropped below normal.

While his friend Rockwell was near his bed on September 18, he asked him, "Do you think my name will have a place in human history?"

Dismayed by the way Garfield asked the question, Rockwell replied, "Yes, a grand one, but a grander one in human hearts. You must not talk in that way. You have a great work yet to perform."

"No," Garfield said in a somber voice, "my work is done."

The next day, September 19, almost two weeks after coming to Elberon, Garfield had an intense chill and a coughing spell, followed by profuse perspiration. He slept most of the day.

At 10:10 that Monday evening, Swaim was on duty in the sleeping president's candlelit room. Suddenly, he heard Garfield gasp. Swaim hurried over to the bed.

Opening his eyes, the president said, "Oh my! Swaim, what a pain I have right here." He placed his hand over his heart.

Garfield fell unconscious. Swaim felt for a pulse but couldn't detect one.

He called for Bliss in the next room. Soon, Lucretia, Mollie, Rockwell, Brown, Agnew, and Boynton rushed into the room and gathered around the bed.

Bliss checked for Garfield's pulse at both his wrist and neck. Nothing. He put his ear to Garfield's chest and heard a faint flutter. The president's skin had lost all color.

"Oh! What is the matter?" Lucretia cried.

"Mrs. Garfield, the President is dying," replied Bliss.

It was the moment Lucretia long feared. She bent down and tenderly kissed her husband's forehead. Then she took his hand in hers.

While the solemn group waited, the president's gasps of breath continued for several more minutes until . . . silence. It was 10:35 p.m.

James Garfield was dead, eighty days after Charles Guiteau's bullet pierced his back.

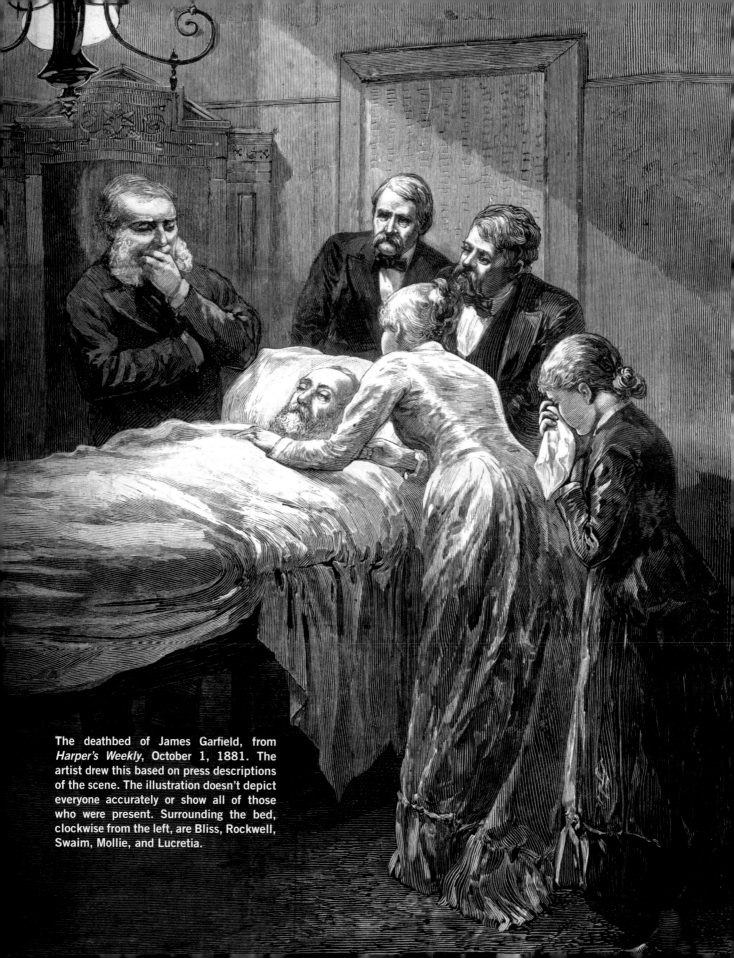

The deathbed of James Garfield, from *Harper's Weekly*, October 1, 1881. The artist drew this based on press descriptions of the scene. The illustration doesn't depict everyone accurately or show all of those who were present. Surrounding the bed, clockwise from the left, are Bliss, Rockwell, Swaim, Mollie, and Lucretia.

CHAPTER THIRTEEN
THE RETURN HOME

"The whole period was one prolonged, hideous nightmare."

—Joseph Stanley Brown

D ESPITE THEIR OVERWHELMING GRIEF, THE MEN AROUND THE bed were aware of their responsibilities. The president was dead, but the U.S. government had to go on.

Brown sent word to the hotel where the cabinet members were staying, and they rushed to Francklyn Cottage. Upon receiving the news, Secretaries Blaine and Lincoln, the only two not in Elberon, took a train from Boston later that night. Brown also telegraphed messages to other key government officials and the Garfield family in Ohio.

Chester Arthur was at his home in New York City. Throughout the previous eighty days, he had kept a low profile. He'd ignored the rumblings from the press and others who were concerned that Garfield was too incapacitated to serve. What will happen, they had said, if the president is still seriously ill when Congress re-adjourns in the fall or if a national emergency occurs? Arthur had refused to discuss taking over Garfield's duties under those circumstances.

When the telegram arrived at his door around midnight, his life suddenly changed. Arthur had been dreading the telegram's arrival for at least half an hour. He'd heard church bells ringing in

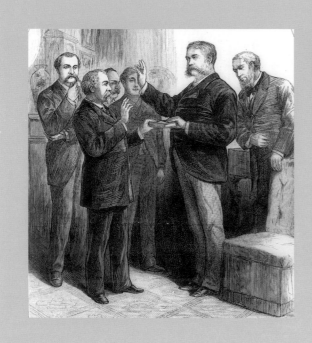

Chester Arthur takes the oath of office in his New York City home on the morning of September 20, 1881. New York Supreme Court Justice John Brady administers the oath. The witnesses included Arthur's seventeen-year-old son and several friends. Two days later, Arthur was given the oath in a short public ceremony at the Capitol by U.S. Supreme Court Chief Justice Morrison Waite. Among the witnesses were cabinet members, some senators and congressmen, and former Presidents Hayes and Grant. This illustration appeared on the front of *Frank Leslie's Illustrated Newspaper*, October 8, 1881.

Manhattan and seen reporters converging on the sidewalk outside his house. He suspected that the worst had happened.

The message from Attorney General Wayne MacVeagh, on behalf of the entire cabinet, informed Arthur that Garfield had died. The vice president was advised to take the oath of office immediately and come to Elberon the next morning.

After a judge was awakened to administer the oath, Arthur and several witnesses gathered in his parlor. At 2:15 in the morning, he became the twenty-first president.

BAD NEWS SPREADS

Overcoming the initial shock of her husband's death, Lucretia summoned the strength she knew was needed to cope with the days ahead. Her composure impressed her children and others around her.

Although Garfield's three older children spent the summer in the White House with their ailing father, they were unprepared for his death. Mollie wrote in her diary, "We all thought darling Papa was on the sure road to recovery, but we were all mistaken."

When her brothers left Washington for Williams College two weeks earlier, they expected their father to regain his health in Elberon. The night of September 19, a messenger came to tell the boys that their father was failing and they were to leave for his bedside as soon as possible. Information traveled slowly from Elberon to the small town of Williamstown, Massachusetts. Hal and Jim didn't learn until the next morning that their papa was already gone.

Taking the first morning train, Hal left on his heartbreaking journey to New Jersey. He traveled alone, because his younger brother was too sick with malaria to go along. Jim had fallen ill a week after arriving at Williams and was fighting high fevers and chills. He would join his family in Ohio a few days later for the funeral and burial, escorted by his closest college friends.

In Elberon and major cities, the word had spread the night before. When cabinet members headed to Francklyn Cottage, reporters realized that Garfield had died. Within a half hour of the president's death, reporters began telegraphing the breaking news to the rest of the nation. By the time Attorney General MacVeagh walked over to the Elberon Hotel and made the official statement to the press, bells were already tolling in city halls, courthouses, churches, and firehouses. In Cleveland, the city that claimed Garfield as its native son, cannons were fired once an hour throughout the night.

On Tuesday, September 20, the sun rose in Elberon over a calm ocean. The morning was clear and warm, a perfect day for a seaside town. But as people there and across the country awoke to headlines and newspaper stories about Garfield's death, most felt sorrow and gloom.

The *Washington Post* proclaimed, "The President Dead. PASSING PEACE-FULLY AWAY LAST EVENING AMIDST FAMILY AND FRIENDS." The headlines of the *Daily Record-Union* in Sacramento, California, dramatically announced, "DEAD. The Long Struggle at Last Ended. DEATH FINALLY PREVAILS."

James Garfield served just two hundred days as president. For eighty of them, he suffered in bed as Americans followed daily reports about his health. They felt as if they knew him intimately, like a family member in the upstairs bedroom struggling to recover from an illness. His death threw the country into mourning. Flags flew at half-mast. Black fabric hung from homes and public buildings.

Newspaper editorials reflected the view of many people. "The President's death will cause less shock, but far more sorrow, than if he had been shot dead on the 2d of July," said the *New York Tribune*. "There has been time to learn that the Government cannot be shaken by the death of any man, however high, or great, or good."

Editorials praised Garfield's courage and intelligence. *Harper's Weekly* called his death "the bitter disappointment of reasonable hopes founded upon his singular fitness for his great office."

Some observers considered Garfield's assassination to be the tragic result of vicious political quarrels. Former President Rutherford Hayes wrote in a letter two weeks after the death, "Perhaps its most important lesson, is the folly, the wickedness, and the danger of the extreme and bitter partisanship which so largely prevails in our country."

The assassin wasn't told of his victim's death that Monday night. But

The funeral train leaves Francklyn Cottage on Wednesday, September 21. The illustration was published in *Harper's Weekly*, October 1, 1881.

Charles Guiteau probably guessed when he heard Washington's pealing bells. After he asked the guards and they confirmed it, Guiteau got on his knees to pray. Only he knew whether the prayers were for the president's soul or for his own life. Now Guiteau would be tried for murder.

Tuesday morning's newspaper articles contained reports of angry cries to drag Guiteau from his cell and hang him on the spot. Although a small group gathered outside the jail on the night of Garfield's death, nothing happened. General William Tecumseh Sherman, in charge of the army, called for order and trust that the legal system would deal with Guiteau.

LAID TO REST

Early Wednesday morning, an undertaker arrived at Francklyn Cottage with a casket. He dressed Garfield's body in the same black coat, vest, and trousers he had worn for his March inauguration. The undertaker was forced to adjust the clothes to fit because the president had lost so much weight since the shooting.

The casket was placed in the hall, and the public was allowed into the cottage to view Garfield's body. At least 1,500 people passed through, many sobbing. After an hour, the doors were shut so that the family, the cabinet, and medical attendants could hold a private religious service.

Afterward, a funeral train pulled up next to the cottage. It was the same one that had brought Garfield to Elberon. His casket was loaded onto a car draped with black cloth. Twelve soldiers rode with the body as an

Headlines of newspapers on Tuesday, September 20, 1881, the morning after Garfield's death. *Daily Gazette*, Wilmington, DE (bottom left); *Las Vegas* [NV] *Daily Gazette* (top); *Wheeling* [WV] *Register* (bottom right)

157

College students at Princeton Junction, New Jersey, placed hundreds of flowers on the tracks to honor the president as the funeral train passed by. Illustration from *Frank Leslie's Illustrated Newspaper*, October 8, 1881

honor guard. The remaining cars carried Garfield's friends, attendants, President Arthur, the cabinet, and family. Hal and Mollie stayed by their mother's side.

Along the route to Washington, the train passed black-draped stations and crowds of mourners standing silently. At Princeton Junction, New Jersey, college students laid flowers on the tracks. The train's wheels crushed the blooms as it slowly passed.

By 5:00 Wednesday evening, the funeral train arrived in Washington. Mollie was worried about how she'd react when she walked through the same room where her father had been shot. But carriages met the train, and no one had to go inside the depot.

A horse-drawn hearse took Garfield's casket to the Capitol, where he had spent seventeen years as a congressman. Thousands stood on the sidewalks to watch it pass.

The White House is draped in black mourning fabric after President Garfield's death.

The casket was opened and placed in the center of the Capitol Rotunda to lie in state. The public was permitted to walk through until Friday at noon, and about 100,000 people filed by Garfield's body.

Those who saw it were shocked by the "shrunken and emaciated features." Despite being embalmed, the body began to decompose and smell by Thursday, three days after Garfield's death. The casket had to be permanently closed.

After a religious service in the Capitol on Friday afternoon, the casket was taken back to the Baltimore and Potomac railroad station. As the funeral train left Washington for Cleveland, warships in the Navy Yard fired their

The illustration from *Harper's Weekly*, October 1, 1881, shows Garfield's casket lying in the Capitol Rotunda. The casket was open for viewing for a while, but was closed when the body began to decompose.

Garfield's coffin on display in Cleveland, Ohio, on September 25, 1881. Britain's Queen Victoria sent the wreath lying on the casket. A quarter-million people walked past to pay their respects. James Blaine stands on the left with bowed head. The image appeared in *Harper's Weekly*, October 8, 1881.

HARPER'S WEEKLY.

JOURNAL OF CIVILIZATION.

Vol. XXV.—No. 1294.
Copyright, 1881, by Harper & Brothers.

FOR THE WEEK ENDING OCTOBER 8, 1881.

TEN CENTS A COPY.
$4.00 PER YEAR, IN ADVANCE.

THE FUNERAL OF PRESIDENT GARFIELD—THE CATAFALQUE AT CLEVELAND.—From Photographs by Liebich and Sketches by Theo. R. Davis.—[See Page 686.]

The James A. Garfield Monument at Lake View Cemetery, Cleveland, Ohio, was dedicated in May 1890. At that time, his casket was moved into the Monument's basement crypt from the vault where it had rested since 1881. The building was constructed using public donations.

After Garfield's death, the public bought numerous commemorative prints. This one shows him with Lucretia and his mother, Eliza. To connect Garfield to the first assassinated president, the illustrator put Abraham Lincoln's portrait on the wall.

guns and bells in the city's churches and schools rang.

Cleveland hosted the final funeral service for President Garfield. The city constructed a large pavilion in a park, and the casket lay on a platform decorated with flowers. By some counts, nearly 250,000 people came to pay their respects, exceeding Cleveland's total population of 160,000.

On Monday morning, September 26, religious services were held at the pavilion and attended by James Garfield's Ohio friends and family as well as by many national dignitaries. A procession of carriages followed the casket to Lake View Cemetery five miles away.

A week after his passing, Garfield was peacefully laid to rest in a vault a few miles from his birthplace. The consequences of his death were yet to come.

Dr. Daniel Lamb (1843–1929) served in military hospitals during the Civil War before obtaining his medical degree in 1867. He was Dr. Woodward's longtime colleague at the Army Medical Museum.

CHAPTER FOURTEEN

THE MISSING BULLET

"We made a mistake."

—Dr. D. Hayes Agnew

J AMES GARFIELD SUFFERED THROUGH MULTIPLE SURGERIES AS his doctors tried and failed to treat his gunshot wound. Before being placed in a casket by the undertaker in Elberon, his body was sliced one final time.

The doctors wanted to learn exactly what killed him. That information was needed as evidence in Charles Guiteau's murder trial. They arranged for an autopsy at Francklyn Cottage, sending for an expert in postmortem examinations.

On Tuesday morning, September 20, Dr. Daniel Lamb of the U.S. Army Medical Museum boarded a train to Elberon from Washington. He'd had fifteen years' experience doing autopsies. Late that afternoon—eighteen hours after the president's death—he made his first incision into Garfield's wasted body.

Observing and assisting with Lamb's autopsy were the six doctors involved in Garfield's case (Bliss, Agnew, Hamilton, Barnes, Reyburn, and Woodward). A local physician attended, too, because state law required a licensed New Jersey doctor to be present. Woodward,

Lamb's colleague from the Medical Museum, took notes of the procedure.

The autopsy lasted more than three hours. A crowd waited outside Francklyn Cottage to hear the results. About 8:00 that evening, Bliss announced to the group that the postmortem showed death was inevitable. He added that this news was a relief to Lucretia.

Several hours later, the doctors released a written summary of the results to the press. The autopsy's findings stunned nearly everyone.

UNEXPECTED

Garfield's doctors had always believed that the bullet traveled down through his abdomen toward his groin. This track, which later filled with pus, extended from the bullet's entrance.

With that in mind, Dr. Lamb began the autopsy by looking for the bullet in the lower abdomen. He pushed aside the intestines and then removed them from the body to be examined further. The bullet wasn't where the doctors expected to find it.

Lamb continued to search inside Garfield's body. When he located the actual path of Guiteau's bullet, the doctors were astonished. It was NOT the channel of pus.

After penetrating Garfield's skin about three and one-half inches to the right of his backbone, the bullet traveled downward and broke the two lowest ribs on his right side.

Deflected to the left by the ribs, the bullet passed through the backbone, damaging bone and cartilage. It did not strike Garfield's spinal cord. The temporary tingling in his feet and legs after the shooting was likely from the initial impact to his backbone.

After exiting a vertebra, the bullet came to rest in fatty tissue behind the pancreas, about two and one-half inches to the left of the backbone. It lay there harmlessly for nearly three months. During that time, the bullet became encased in a layer of scar tissue. The surrounding area healed.

Young Dr. Frank Baker's hypothesis, which he proposed two days after the assassination, had been correct. Guiteau's bullet traveled into the left side of Garfield's body, not down the right as his doctors thought.

The autopsy report claimed that the channel of pus formed as a result of infection caused by the tiny splintered bones broken off by the bullet. That infection, the report said, eventually entered the bloodstream and spread throughout the president's body.

Further examination of Garfield's organs revealed that none was hit by the bullet. His liver hadn't been struck as the doctors initially believed. The president's lungs, however, showed that he developed pneumonia near the end of his life.

When Agnew saw the damaged backbone, he stuck his little finger through the hole created by Guiteau's bullet. "Gentlemen," he said to the group gathered around Garfield's body, "this was the fatal wound. We made a mistake."

Lamb and the other doctors concluded that, besides barreling through a vertebra, the bullet grazed an artery near the pancreas. The torn edges of the artery's walls formed a bulging sac that held in

The photograph of part of James Garfield's backbone shows the track of the bullet, indicated with the red dowel. These vertebrae and the bullet were shown to the jury as evidence during Guiteau's trial. This section of backbone is stored at the National Museum of Health and Medicine in Silver Spring, Maryland.

blood flowing through the vessel. In their report, the doctors blamed Garfield's death on the bursting of this sac. He felt pain in his lower chest, they said, when the artery's blood escaped into his abdominal cavity.

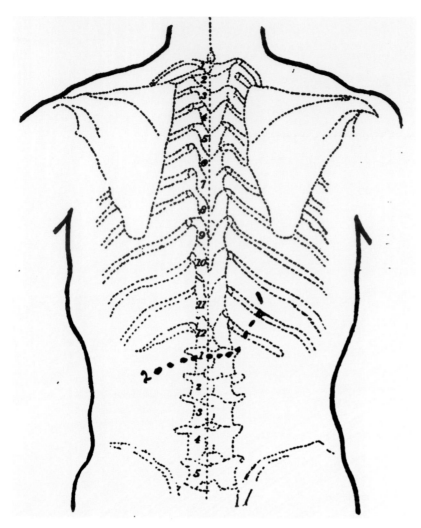

This drawing of Garfield's back shows where the bullet entered his body, labeled "1"; the dotted line of its path through the backbone; and where it landed, labeled "2." The illustration was published in a book by Dr. Reyburn.

They believed the autopsy proved that the bullet wound had been fatal from the beginning. Even if the doctors had known about its damage, surgery to fix a blood vessel or remove a bullet deep in the body wasn't possible in 1881. Garfield had no chance of recovering.

Several years later, Dr. Reyburn wrote that the surgeons were wrong about the bullet's path, but "no different course of treatment could have saved his life." Even without the artery sac bursting, Garfield would have ultimately died from the severe blood infection caused by the pieces of broken bone. That infection, Reyburn wrote, was first obvious around July 23 when Garfield began having chills and high fever. As the infection spread through his body, it "could only result in inevitable death."

AUTOPSY CHALLENGED

As soon as the autopsy results were published, they were disputed. Some in the medical community didn't accept the conclusion that a ruptured artery killed

Garfield. If the blood vessel was injured at the time of the shooting, they argued, the sac would have burst long before eighty days passed. Others believed that the artery had been damaged by the overwhelming infection, not the bullet.

Critics noted that the presence of embalming liquid could have led to inaccurate conclusions. Hours before the doctors began the autopsy, embalming fluid was injected into Garfield's circulatory system in order to stop his body from decomposing too fast. Some suggested that the liquid itself ruptured the artery sac.

Others proposed that Garfield's chest pain shortly before death was more likely the result of a blood clot in his heart. Lamb may have failed to find this clot because of changes caused by the embalming process.

Additional questions concerned the bullet's resting place. It had not been spotted *inside* Garfield's body during the postmortem. The doctors found it among blood and tissue cut out and moved to a basin for examination. That raised doubts about the reliability of the autopsy.

"IGNORANCE IS BLISS"

For weeks before Garfield's death, medical journals and general newspapers had accused Bliss of mismanaging his care. A Kentucky newspaper published one such dig at Bliss's handling of the case: "The people of the United States never fully appreciated the force of the aphorism 'Ignorance is Bliss,' until President Garfield was shot."

Now the attacks on Bliss and the other doctors grew louder. Some physicians said there was nothing inevitable about Garfield's death from the bullet wound. They charged that Bliss was more concerned about protecting his reputation than admitting the obvious truth: The body of a forty-nine-year-old man in previous good health had been destroyed by infection and starvation.

Boynton disapproved of his cousin's treatment throughout the ordeal.

After the death, he argued that Garfield had a chance of recovering if his wound had been cleaned correctly in the beginning. Boynton praised Drs. Agnew and Hamilton. But in his opinion, by the time the two surgeons operated on Garfield three weeks after the shooting, the harm was done. Infection had entered Garfield's bloodstream.

Several surgeons with gunshot wound experience declared that damage to the vertebrae and ribs alone would not cause death. The pus channel and blood infection were not the result of these injuries. Instead, Garfield's bullet wound had been contaminated with bacteria by his own doctors, starting with the first examination on the dirty floor of the railroad depot.

These critics charged that Garfield's physicians followed outdated Civil War era medical ideas. Because Bliss and the others didn't accept Lister's principles of infection, they provided flawed care.

Bliss forcefully disagreed. He and the medical team had followed the best antiseptic guidelines for dressings and treatment.

No, the detractors responded. The fact that Garfield's doctors inserted unwashed fingers into the bullet wound proved that they had NOT followed Lister's antiseptic methods. If they hadn't continually searched for the bullet with germ-laden fingers and probes, the president probably would have survived. James Garfield had been attacked first by Guiteau and then by bacteria.

Supporters of Garfield's doctors rushed to their defense, saying that the negative comments were not based on direct observation of the patient or of the autopsy. It was unprofessional of other doctors to make such attacks. Because of the expertise of Garfield's doctors, wrote one physician, "A very valuable life was prolonged beyond all reasonable hope." No one could have saved the president.

A newspaper editorial noted: "The fact that the president lived for seventy-nine days after wounded, as known now, will always be remarked as one of the most remarkable triumphs of medical skill."

During the 140 years since Garfield's death, medical experts have reviewed the record and offered their opinions about his treatment. But Garfield's case is difficult to analyze based on historical documents alone. His doctors' daily medical bulletins were often intentionally misleading.

The postmortem was not performed with modern precision, and it was controversial even at the time.

Still, many experts have concluded that Garfield's wound was not necessarily fatal, even given the limits of 1881 medical technology and knowledge. He might have survived if the doctors simply allowed his body to heal on its own. On a single point, most modern physicians agree. The constant probing with unsterilized fingers and instruments introduced bacteria that the president's body was unable to fight.

In 1881, the criticisms about Garfield's medical treatment weren't lost on one man. Charles Guiteau hoped the doctors' mistakes would save his life.

The cover of *Puck* depicts Garfield's doctors leaving Francklyn Cottage after the autopsy: Bliss, Agnew, Hamilton, Reyburn, Woodward. The men hold pieces of paper that read "Self-Exoneration." The illustrator added this because the autopsy report concluded that Garfield's wound was fatal from the start and that his doctors had no chance of saving his life. The three men on the left represent ideas for treating the president that were not followed by his medical team.

Where Justice Will Have to Look for Jurors Who Have Not Formed an Opinion in the Guiteau Case.

CHAPTER FIFTEEN

THE TRIAL

"We say that his death was caused by malpractice.
That is all there is to it."

—Charles Guiteau

T EN DAYS AFTER HER FATHER'S DEATH, MOLLIE GARFIELD WROTE IN her diary, "I suspect I am wicked but these are my feelings; Guiteau ought to be made to suffer as much and a thousand times more than Papa did."

She wasn't the only one who felt that way.

For eighty days, anxious Americans consumed every detail about President Garfield's medical condition. Now, as they mourned his death, people across the country demanded justice, and they wanted it fast. Within two months of Garfield's death, Guiteau's trial began.

Newspapers sprang into action, supplying readers with the information they craved. The Washington trial became a media spectacle. Reporters wrote about the court proceedings and dug up background about Guiteau, the lawyers, and the witnesses who testified. The daily newspapers provided stories, but they didn't yet have the technology to print photographs.

According to this *Puck* illustration, it would be impossible to find a living person to serve as a juror who did not know about the assassination and had not already decided that Guiteau was guilty.

Instead, the weekly illustrated newspapers and magazines published drawings produced by their own artists. The public had to wait at least a week to see these images from the trial.

Anyone eager to watch the historic event in person obtained an admission ticket from District Attorney Corkhill's office. Harriet Blaine was one Washington resident who attended, going at least three times. She was willing to sit in a cramped, suffocating courtroom for several hours to see the proceedings against "as dreadful a villain as civilization has produced." She called the trial "the most interesting place, by all odds, in Washington."

HARPER'S WEEKLY.

JOURNAL OF CIVILIZATION.

Vol. XXV.—No. 1302.
Copyright, 1881, by Harper & Brothers.

FOR THE WEEK ENDING DECEMBER 3, 1881.

TEN CENTS A COPY.
$4.00 PER YEAR, IN ADVANCE.

DISTRICT ATTORNEY CORKHILL.
PHOTOGRAPHED BY BELL.

PRESIDING JUDGE WALTER S. COX.
PHOTOGRAPHED BY BELL.

GEORGE M. SCOVILLE.
PHOTOGRAPHED BY BELL.

The first page of *Harper's Weekly*, December 3, 1881, included illustrations of George Corkhill, Washington's district attorney, who prosecuted Charles Guiteau; the judge, Walter Cox; and attorney George Scoville, Guiteau's brother-in-law, who defended him.

THE PROSECUTION

The charge against Guiteau was the intentional, premeditated murder of James Garfield with a pistol and lead bullet. After authorization by President Arthur and the cabinet, Attorney General MacVeagh added two prominent trial attorneys to the prosecution team to assist Corkhill, who was a less-experienced criminal lawyer. The conviction of Guiteau could not be left to chance.

By November 17, 1881, the jury had been selected and sworn in. District Attorney Corkhill told the twelve men (women did not serve on juries) that Guiteau carefully planned his attack on Garfield and acted with a motive. Despite claims to the contrary, Corkhill said, the assassin was completely sane.

The prosecution set out to prove its case to the jurors. Corkhill called witnesses to testify about Guiteau's actions before the shooting, his attack at the train station, his arrest, and the president's medical condition.

The district attorney produced notes that Guiteau had sent to Garfield and Secretary of State Blaine. In these, Guiteau revealed his indignation at being refused a job in the new administration. Joseph Stanley Brown was called to testify about the assassin's visits to the White House. Corkhill presented Guiteau's letters addressed to the American people, written before the assassination, in which he explained his plan and motive for killing the president. The jury was shown the murder weapon and heard testimony from the store owner who sold it to Guiteau.

Railroad employees, policemen, travelers, and Garfield associates (including Blaine and Almon Rockwell) described what they saw on July 2 at the train station. Several of the witnesses identified Charles Guiteau as Garfield's attacker.

A boisterous crowd gathers outside the Washington courthouse on November 14, 1881, the first day of the trial. Some are trying to get inside to watch the proceedings. Others hope for a glimpse of Guiteau as he arrives by police wagon from his jail cell. Many are there to voice their outrage at his shooting of Garfield. From *Harper's Weekly*, November 26, 1881

Drs. Barnes and Woodward both stated under oath that the bullet wound was the cause of the president's death. Dr. Lamb testified that the wound had been a mortal one from which the president couldn't have recovered. Lamb produced the bullet, removed from the body during the autopsy, and it was shown to the jury.

When Dr. Bliss took the witness stand, he was questioned by both the district attorney and Guiteau's lawyer about Garfield's medical care from the day of the shooting until his death. The gunshot had been fatal, Bliss testified, and the autopsy proved Garfield had no chance of surviving.

Using diagrams, Bliss explained to the jury how the bullet passed through the president's body. The district attorney presented Garfield's damaged vertebrae, and Bliss pointed out where the bullet penetrated the backbone.

THE DEFENSE

For most of the trial, George Scoville handled his brother-in-law's defense alone. Scoville, who practiced law in Illinois, wasn't a criminal attorney. Although he'd attempted to get assistance from an experienced trial lawyer, no one was willing to help represent Guiteau. Finally, more than a month into the trial, a Chicago criminal lawyer who was Scoville's friend agreed to join the defense team.

Guiteau insisted that incompetent doctors had killed Garfield. But Scoville thought the best chance to save Guiteau was to show that he had been born with mental defects and was insane. For that reason, he couldn't be held responsible for his actions.

In his opening statement to the jury, Scoville attributed the assassin's actions to a disturbed mind. "Guiteau never had anything to do with the construction of his brain," Scoville said. "If it is not properly constructed, if it is not right, if there is some defect there, it is not his fault."

By presenting evidence about the mental state of Guiteau's kin, Scoville tried to prove that insanity ran in the family. The attorney offered letters written by Guiteau that demonstrated his erratic and often irrational behavior, starting from childhood. Scoville put acquaintances and relatives on the witness stand to describe the defendant's odd conduct.

Dozens of psychiatrists testified. Was Guiteau insane and unable to control his actions? Or was he sane, fully understanding the consequences of shooting Garfield? The experts didn't agree.

Guiteau's courtroom rants and outbursts certainly made him seem mentally disturbed. Frequently jumping from his chair, he interrupted and verbally attacked witnesses, the prosecution attorneys, the judge, and even Scoville. During some witness testimonies, Guiteau made a show of ignoring the speaker on the stand by reading his newspapers and brushing away flies around his head.

Continued on page 178

An illustration in *Harper's Weekly*, December 3, 1881, shows the courtroom. The space was renovated to accommodate the many reporters and spectators interested in attending the famous trial. Observers and trial participants were labeled, including Charles Guiteau's sister, Frances, (#2) and her daughter; Guiteau (#9); George Scoville (#10); reporters and artists (#17); and the *Harper's Weekly* artist (#16), who drew himself in the foreground sketching on a pad.

After court adjourned on Saturday afternoon, November 19, at the end of the trial's first week, the handcuffed Guiteau was hustled into the police van for the drive back to the jail. As the wagon passed the Capitol, a shot rang out. A man on horseback had fired into the van. The bullet ripped through Guiteau's coat but missed his body.

The police gave chase, and a young farmer named William Jones was arrested. He was released on bond and never brought to trial. Many people hailed Jones as a hero. Critics said that government officials weren't being careful enough in guarding Guiteau. The illustration appeared in *Harper's Weekly*, December 3, 1881.

But his case for insanity was damaged when his former wife, Annie, was called to the witness stand by the prosecution. District Attorney Corkhill addressed her. "I will ask you to state to the jury whether, in your association with him, you ever saw anything that would indicate that he was a man of unsound mind?"

She replied, "I never did."

STAR WITNESS

The trial's most riveting witness was Charles Guiteau himself.

He admitted shooting James Garfield. He had no choice. God picked him for the task. "I was doing the work of the Lord," he told the courtroom. Guiteau was proud of his actions. "I was the only man throughout the entire nation," he bragged, "that had the inspiration and the nerve and the brain and the opportunity to do the work."

From the witness stand, Guiteau explained that he bought the gun in order "to remove the President for the good of the American people." He recounted how he stalked Garfield before the July 2 attack, testifying that he "intended to execute the divine will." But, he said, "I think the doctors did the work." In one courtroom outburst, Guiteau stated, "I deny the killing, if your honor please; we admit the shooting."

THE JURY DECIDES

The trial lasted until the end of January 1882, and about 150 people testified
as witnesses. Late in the afternoon of Wednesday, January 25, Judge Walter
Cox turned the case over to the jury. He spent nearly an hour and a half
instructing the jurors about the decision they would be making.

Because all the surgeons had testified that the bullet wound was mortal,
Cox said, doctor malpractice was not an issue in determining the defendant's
guilt. The judge explained that the jury must decide whether Guiteau was
sane when he shot Garfield. Was he capable of telling right from wrong?
"If you should think that the prisoner is not guilty by reason of insanity, it is
proper for you to say so."

By 4:35, the winter day was slipping into darkness. Candles were lit in
the courthouse as the jury left the room to decide Guiteau's fate.

After less than an hour of deliberations, the twelve men returned to the courtroom.

The court clerk asked, "Gentlemen of the jury, have you agreed upon a verdict?"

The jury foreman answered, "We have."

"What say you? Is the defendant guilty or not guilty?"

"Guilty as indicted, sir," replied the foreman.

The clerk asked each juror the same question. One at a time, they responded, "Guilty."

Guiteau called out, "My blood be on the head of that jury; don't you forget it. That is my answer."

Ten days later, Judge Cox announced his sentence, speaking directly to Guiteau. He would remain in jail until June 30, 1882, said Cox, at which time he would "be hung by the neck until you shall be dead; and may God have mercy upon your soul."

Guiteau shouted at the judge, "God Almighty will curse every man who has had anything to do with this case. Don't you forget that."

Guiteau is led away after the verdict on January 25, 1882. Men shake their fists and canes at him, showing their anger at the convicted assassin. The illustration appeared in a book about the trial proceedings published later that year.

FAREWELL

The verdict was cheered by observers in the courtroom, the crowd outside the courthouse, and most Americans who read about it. Justice had finally been done. Harriet Blaine expressed the opinion of many when she said, "I have but one wish, to see him put out of the way. I want it impossible for that hoarse, cracked voice, ever to raise itself again."

Some people, however, criticized the trial and the verdict as inhumane. Guiteau was clearly insane, they said. Insane individuals should be put in mental asylums, not put to death. The jury's lightning-quick decision showed that the public sentiment to hang Guiteau had sealed his fate even before the trial began.

Charles J. Guiteau

Guiteau was photographed in jail in early February 1882, after a jury found him guilty of murder. His attorney appealed the decision, but the jury's verdict held.

Scoville appealed the verdict, requesting a new trial. During the next several months, Guiteau and his family attempted to obtain a pardon, going as far as sending their request to President Arthur. Their efforts failed, and Judge Cox's sentence stood.

By noon on Friday, June 30, 1882, 250 reporters and officials stood in the prison courtyard in front of a scaffold, waiting for Guiteau to appear. Almost 2,000 more people—men women, and children—crowded outside the jail walls under overcast skies.

That morning, Guiteau took a bath, put on a respectable suit, and had his shoes shined. Around 12:30 p.m., prison officials led him from his cell to the courtyard and up the scaffold steps.

Standing above the crowd with his arms tied behind his back, he loudly read his dying prayer from a paper held in front of him by a clergyman. Near the end of the prayer, which Guiteau had written earlier in the day, he said,

A sketch of the hanging of Charles Guiteau on June 30, 1882, appeared in *Frank Leslie's Illustrated Newspaper*, July 8, 1882. A crowd was on hand for the event. Guiteau's body was placed in a coffin, and for about twenty minutes before the autopsy was performed, spectators at the jail were allowed to file past and view it.

"Arthur, the President, is a coward and an ingrate . . . but Thou, Righteous Father, will judge him. . . . Farewell, ye men of earth."

Then the convicted assassin chanted verses he had composed a few hours before. "Glory Hallelujah! I am going to the Lordy." Partway through the stanzas, he began to sob.

The executioner lowered the noose around Guiteau's neck and covered his head with a black hood.

Guiteau shouted, "Glory, glory, glory!"

Click. The trapdoor sprung open. Guiteau dropped through the opening, his limp body hanging from the noose.

It was two days before the one-year anniversary of Guiteau's attack on President Garfield. Now Charles and James were both dead.

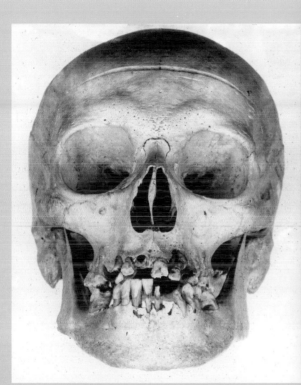 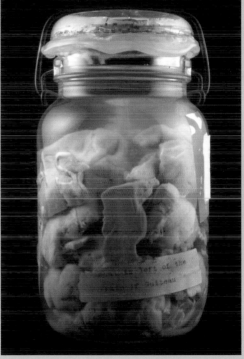

Less than two hours after Guiteau died, an autopsy was performed on his body at the jail by Dr. Daniel Lamb, who had also done the postmortem on James Garfield. Lamb sent parts of Guiteau's body to the U.S. Army Medical Museum—now the National Museum of Health and Medicine. The Museum still has portions of his brain (shown in a jar, right), most of his skeleton, and his spleen. His skull (left) is no longer with the rest of the skeleton in the Museum's collection, and its location is a mystery. Except for his enlarged spleen, a sign of a malaria infection, Guiteau's body revealed nothing unusual.

Lucretia Garfield, photographed several months before the assassination. In her later years, she lived most of the time in Pasadena, California, where she died in March 1918, a month before her eighty-sixth birthday.

CHAPTER SIXTEEN

THE REST OF THE STORY

"It seems so so cruel to think that he, such true & noble Christian, should have to suffer so & at last die, when there was no reason."

—Mollie Garfield

WHAT HAPPENED TO . . . ?

James Garfield's Family

Each member of Garfield's family profoundly missed his presence and influence. But thanks to the fund begun by Cyrus Field after the July shooting, Lucretia didn't have to worry about supporting her family without her husband's income. Donations to the Garfield Fund totaled $360,000, an amount equal to more than $9,000,000 today. Congress granted Lucretia an additional pension of $5,000 a year, a sum also paid to other widowed first ladies.

With part of the money, Lucretia enlarged the house at Lawnfield in Mentor, where Garfield's

Lucretia had sixteen grandchildren. Here, she poses with most of them in 1906.

mother and Lucretia's father lived with the family. Lucretia's brother, Joseph Rudolph, and his family moved in to assist with the farm. The addition to the house included the Memorial Library to keep most of Garfield's five thousand books. A fireproof vault in the library stored his diaries, papers, and memorabilia such as the funeral wreath sent by Britain's Queen Victoria.

Joseph Stanley-Brown (who added a hyphen to his name) spent eighteen months helping Lucretia organize the former president's papers. The family gave the extensive collection to the Library of Congress nearly fifty years later.

In appreciation for what Stanley-Brown had done for the president and the family, Lucretia helped pay for his education at Yale College in Connecticut. He spent his career in government, railroads, and banking.

With the money in the fund, Lucretia was able to support the education

This painting, "The Agnew Clinic," by Thomas Eakins, shows Dr. D. Hayes Agnew (on the left) during a surgical demonstration before medical students at the University of Pennsylvania. It was created in 1889 in honor of Agnew's retirement. The painting shows the changes brought about by the wide acceptance of germ theory and Lister's antiseptic methods. The doctors wear white gowns and the patient lies on clean linens. But at this time, surgeons still did not follow most of the procedures used in today's operating rooms to prevent infection. They did not wear gloves, masks, or caps over their hair. Surgeries were often performed in a room with other people in street clothes sitting or standing close to the patient.

Protecting the President

Despite Abraham Lincoln's assassination just sixteen years earlier, President Garfield did not have armed guards protecting him. Neither had any other president after Lincoln.

When Guiteau attacked, editorial writers and others called for full-time protection of the president. Even though Garfield died from his bullet wound, this change did not happen until after the 1901 assassination of President William McKinley. Then, Congress assigned the duty of guarding the president to the U.S. Secret Service, which was already responsible for defending the government against fraud and counterfeiting.

Since 1901, numerous assassination attempts have been made on presidents. Three resulted in physical harm, all by gunshot. Former President Theodore Roosevelt suffered a non-life-threatening chest wound in 1912. President John Kennedy was shot and killed in 1963.

The third occurred in 1981, one hundred years after Garfield's assassination. On March 30, twenty-five-year-old John Hinckley stepped from a group of reporters on the sidewalk outside a Washington hotel and shot six times at President Ronald Reagan. One bullet hit Reagan in the chest. Hinckley wounded three others that day—Reagan's press secretary (who was permanently disabled by a bullet to his head), a Secret Service agent, and a police officer. The shooter was tackled within seconds.

Two Secret Service agents shoved Reagan into the presidential limousine, which sped to a nearby emergency room where the president received immediate life-saving treatment. Within an hour of the shooting, he was in surgery. The bullet missed his heart by barely an inch, but it punctured a lung. Reagan lost more than half his body's blood.

During nearly three hours of surgery, doctors treated his lung injury, removed the bullet, and controlled his bleeding. The president received antibiotics to fight possible infection and transfusions to replace his significant blood loss.

Within two weeks, Reagan walked out of the hospital and returned to the White House. He eventually made a full recovery. His wound was far more serious than Garfield's, and without emergency treatment, Reagan would have died.

President Reagan's attacker, like Charles Guiteau, had a history of mental illness. Hinckley was tried and found not guilty by reason of insanity. He was sent to a psychiatric hospital rather than to the gallows.

The Tragic Loss

Today, emergency room physicians would save James Garfield. Strict procedures would be followed to prevent new bacteria from infecting his body. All medical instruments and wound dressings would be sterile.

To prevent shock and infection, he would be given fluids and antibiotics intravenously through a sterile tube and needle directly into his bloodstream. By measuring his blood pressure, oxygen levels, and heart and breathing rates, doctors would get valuable information about the extent of his wound.

This monument to Garfield has stood near the U.S. Capitol in Washington since 1887.

James Garfield, in an 1881 print published after his death

They could use X-rays, CT scans, and MRIs to locate the bullet, reveal the damage to his ribs and vertebrae, and show that his organs and spinal cord were uninjured.

Since Garfield didn't lose much blood, he wouldn't need a transfusion. His broken ribs and vertebrae would likely heal without surgery. Antibiotics would stop any infection that might result from the broken bones, the bullet, or the clothing fibers driven into the wound.

Because no vital body parts had been damaged and the bullet was lying harmlessly in fatty tissue, it wouldn't necessarily have to be removed. But if tests showed that the bullet could be extracted without damaging nerves or organs, Garfield might undergo surgery. The operating room and surgical instruments would be germ-free. Doctors and nurses would wear sterile gowns, gloves, shoe covers, caps over their hair, and masks over their noses and mouths.

Doctors would keep Garfield in the hospital for several days to watch for unforeseen complications. After that, the president could recuperate in the White House. He'd probably return to work within a few weeks.

Sadly, James Garfield didn't receive these treatments.

The promises of his presidency were dashed on the morning of July 2, 1881. Despite his many contributions as a congressman, Garfield never accomplished his goals for the nation or himself. He never achieved greatness in the history books. But the tragic fiasco leading to his death helped propel the American medical community into the next century. And that has saved countless lives from the ravages of deadly infections.

A print published in early 1882 and sold to the public as a keepsake in memory of James Garfield. His middle name, Abram, was misspelled.

GEN. JAMES ABRAHAM GARFIELD K.T. 14° A & A. S.R.

LATE PRESIDENT U.S.A.

The Garfield family, published with Lucretia's permission in December 1881. (Sitting left to right): Abe, Lucretia, President Garfield, Irv, and Garfield's mother, Eliza. (Standing left to right) Jim, Mollie, and Hal

GLOSSARY

abscess: a swelling caused by a collection of pus.

amputation: surgical removal of a limb.

anesthetic: a drug that stops a patient from feeling pain during surgery.

antibiotic: a drug used to destroy disease causing bacteria.

antiseptic: preventing the growth of microbes; a substance that prevents microbe growth.

autopsy (postmortem): the examination of a body to determine cause of death.

bacteria: microscopic one-celled organisms.

cadaver: a dead human body.

carbolic acid: a chemical used to prevent infection.

cholera: a disease caused by bacteria. Symptoms include severe diarrhea.

CT (computed tomography) **scan:** a method of creating detailed images of internal body structures by using radiation.

dark horse: an unexpected winner.

diarrhea: an intestinal ailment in which bowel movements are watery and frequent.

diphtheria: a disease caused by bacteria. Symptoms include sore throat, fever, difficulty breathing, damage to organs.

dressing: a protective covering made of soft cloth, such as a gauze pad, placed over a wound.

dysentery: an intestinal disease with symptoms of abdominal pain, vomiting, and severe, often bloody diarrhea.

enema: injection of liquid into the intestinal system by way of the anus.

feces: body waste discharged from the intestines.

germ theory: the idea that diseases can be caused by microorganisms.

groin: area of the body between the upper thigh and lower abdomen.

infectious disease: an illness caused by an organism such as a bacterium, virus, or parasite that invades the body.

jaundice: yellowing of the skin and eyes, often a sign of liver dysfunction.

malaria: an infectious disease caused by parasitic microbes transmitted by mosquitoes. Symptoms include fever and chills. Occurs in wet areas where mosquitoes breed.

miasma: foul-smelling fumes coming from decomposing plant or animal material; once believed to cause disease.

microbe, or **microorganism**: a microscopic organism, such as a bacterium or virus.

morphine: an addictive drug derived from opium that induces sleep and dulls pain.

MRI (magnetic resonance imaging): a method of creating pictures of the inside of the body without using radiation.

opium: an addictive drug made from poppies that relieves pain and produces sleep.

pancreas: an organ that aids in digestion.

pelvis: the hip area of the human body.

plague: a deadly disease caused by a bacterium. Symptoms include swollen lymph nodes, infected lungs, and blood poisoning.

pneumonia: lung infection with symptoms of cough, chest pain, rapid breathing, and fever.

pus: fluid formed during an infection. It consists of bacteria mixed with dead white blood cells and tissue.

rectum: the lowest part of the large intestine, which connects to the anus.

shock: a medical condition that occurs when blood flow throughout the body is reduced; symptoms include a rapid heartbeat, shallow breathing, sweating.

tuberculosis: a serious and sometimes fatal lung disease caused by a bacterium. Symptoms may include cough, chest pain, fever, fatigue, and weight loss.

typhoid fever: an infectious disease caused by a bacterium that spreads through food and water contaminated with body waste. Symptoms include high fever, headache, reddish skin spots, and bleeding from intestines.

urine: body waste discharged from the kidneys.

vaccine: a special preparation of killed or weakened microbes that triggers the body to produce immunity to a disease.

vertebra: a segment of the backbone.

virus: a minute particle composed of a protein shell containing genetic material. It often causes disease when it invades living cells.

whooping cough (pertussis): a contagious disease caused by bacteria. Symptoms include runny nose, fever, severe cough. Resulting pneumonia can lead to death.

The two Republican candidates in a campaign poster from the 1880 presidential campaign.

TIMELINE

Garfield in 1880

1861-65
American Civil War

1861
Garfield passes the Ohio bar exam.

1860-65
Guiteau lives in Oneida Community, New York.

1860-61
Garfield serves in Ohio State Senate.

1858
Garfield marries Lucretia Rudolph.

1856-61
Garfield is teacher and president of Eclectic Institute.

1854-56
Garfield studies at Williams College in Massachusetts.

1831
November 19
James Garfield born in Ohio.

1851-54
Garfield studies at Western Reserve Eclectic Institute in Ohio.

1849-51
Garfield studies at Geauga Seminary in Ohio.

1841
September 8
Charles Guiteau born in Illinois.

1861-63
Garfield serves as a U.S. Army officer.

1863-80
Garfield serves as U.S. congressman from Ohio.

1865
April 15
Abraham Lincoln dies from assassination.

1865-69
Presidency of Andrew Johnson

1867
Joseph Lister publishes his research on antiseptic surgery.

1868
Guiteau gets law license in Illinois.

1869-77
Presidency of Ulysses Grant

1876
Lister lectures in the U.S. about antiseptic medical care.

1877-81
Presidency of Rutherford Hayes

1880
November 2
Garfield elected 20th President of the United States.

1881
March 4
Garfield inaugurated.

March 5
Guiteau comes to Washington.

June 8
Guiteau buys a gun.

July 2
Guiteau shoots Garfield and is arrested.

July 11
Air-cooling equipment set up in White House.

July 24
Garfield undergoes first surgery to drain pus from bullet wound.

August 1
Alexander Graham Bell fails to locate bullet with his device.

September 6
Garfield is moved to Elberon, New Jersey.

September 19
Garfield dies.

September 20
Chester Arthur becomes president.

November 17
Guiteau's trial begins.

1882
January 25
Guiteau convicted of murder.

June 30
Guiteau hanged.

MORE TO EXPLORE*

*Websites active at time of publication

American Experience: Murder of a President. Directed by Rob Rapley. PBS and WGBH Educational Foundation, 2016.
pbs.org/wgbh/americanexperience/films/garfield
Watch the *American Experience* episode about the Garfield assassination. The online companion provides a program transcript and links to information about Garfield's life, his family, presidential protection, and assassinations.

James A. Garfield National Historic Site, Mentor, Ohio.
National Park Service.
nps.gov/jaga
The U.S. National Park Service provides tours of Garfield's home and farm. The visitor center features informational displays and special programs. The website contains videos, articles, photographs, and links to more information.

James A. Garfield Papers, Library of Congress.
loc.gov/collections/james-a-garfield-papers/about-this-collection
Visit the Library of Congress website to access online resources about Garfield's private life, the 1880 presidential election, and his presidency. Read his diaries, speeches, and letters to family.

First Ladies Lucretia Garfield and Mary Arthur McElroy
C-Span.
c-span.org/video/?310737-1/ladies-lucretia-garfield-mary-arthur-mcelroy
Learn about Lucretia Garfield, her family, and her life as a widow. Watch
narrated videos from the James A. Garfield National Historic Site showing
the interior of the Mentor home decorated as it appeared in 1881. Take a
look inside the first presidential memorial library, established after Garfield's
death by Lucretia to store her husband's papers and books.
The second part of the video discusses the first lady during Chester Arthur's
administration—his sister Mary Arthur McElroy.

U. S. Secret Service.
SecretService.gov
Find out about the history of the Secret Service, including how the agency's
protection duties have expanded over the years. Read about other
presidential assassinations.

Alexander Graham Bell Family Papers, Library of Congress.
**loc.gov/collections/alexander-graham-bell-papers/
about-this-collection**
Learn about Alexander Graham Bell, his invention of the telephone, and his
other scientific work. View photographs and his laboratory notebooks. Read
Bell's letters to family, friends, and business associates. Check out the
Articles and Essays section for more about his life and inventions. The
Related Resources section has links to books and websites.

National Constitution Center.
constitutioncenter.org/learn/hall-pass
Watch videos in which Constitution experts explain the Thirteenth and
Fourteenth Amendments. Congress passed these two amendments, along
with the Fifteenth, while Garfield served in the House of Representatives.

J. A. Garfield.

Born November 19th, 1831.   Died September 19th, 1881.

AUTHOR'S NOTE

The human body is in a never-ending war with harmful microbes—even when we don't know what the enemy is. James Garfield became a casualty in that battle as much as he was the victim of Charles Guiteau's bullet.

Garfield's assassination occurred during a critical period in medicine. The germ theory had been proposed, and some doctors were already using antiseptic approaches. Yet many in the American medical community did not understand nor accept the connection between microbes and disease. That ignorance turned Garfield's injury into a medical fiasco.

The story behind the assassination and Garfield's slow decline to death was more difficult to research than I expected. Truth and myth had become tangled and were often tricky to sort out. In writing this book, I have done my best to give an accurate account.

I began my research with an overview by reading books and academic articles about Garfield's rise to the presidency, his assassination, and his medical case.

My visit to the James A. Garfield National Historic Site in Mentor, Ohio, helped to bring the man to life. I walked through his Lawnfield farmhouse and saw his books, desk, and other family belongings. I stood on the porch where he addressed thousands of well-wishers during his 1880 presidential campaign. During that visit, I listened to a lecture about the assassination and its relevance to another medical fiasco (the Civil War) by Jake Wynn, of the National Museum of Civil War Medicine, in Frederick, Maryland.

Next I turned to primary sources, including diaries, letters, and interviews. All scenes and direct quotations in this book are based on first-person narratives by people who were present. I tried to find material written at the time, not months or years later after memories had faded. Diaries and personal letters are always revealing and usually unguarded, especially if the author expected his or her thoughts and opinions to remain private. In using these sources, however, I considered the perspective and motivations of the writer.

The Library of Congress has digitized James Garfield's papers, including both his private and public writings. I also used the works of other eyewitnesses to Garfield's life and death, including his wife, children, and friends. Charles Guiteau told his story in interviews, an autobiography, and court testimony.

Several of Garfield's doctors discussed the president's case in interviews, articles, and their testimony at Guiteau's trial. For additional specifics, I referred to the daily medical bulletins and the autopsy. In 1894, Dr. Robert Reyburn wrote a more candid description of Garfield's treatment after the other physicians on Bliss's handpicked medical team had died.

On July 2, 1881, there were no cameras to record the assassination. To track down the details of the event, I relied on eyewitness reports. The official record of Guiteau's trial was useful because witnesses testified under oath. Even so, people who had been at the train station told differing stories of what happened. Their accounts depended on how observant they were, where they stood, and when they glanced toward the shooter.

Some versions were wrong. For example, according to Jim Garfield's diary written that day, he and his brother did not see the shooting. But a few witnesses claimed the boys did, probably because the two appeared beside their father moments later.

With no existing photographs of Garfield's shooting, sickroom, transfer to Elberon, or funeral, I examined illustrations. I determined which drawings fit eyewitness descriptions and which were based on the artist's imagination.

By reviewing newspapers and news magazines from the summer of 1881, I learned what Americans knew of the tragedy. By reading the telegrams and letters they sent to Garfield (available at the Library of Congress), I found out how the public felt about it.

Not all news reports were reliable. To determine their accuracy, I searched for corroboration in multiple newspapers and in statements by eyewitnesses. According to Drs. Robert Reyburn and Silas Boynton, some information given to the press, such as the doctors' daily medical bulletins, was misleading. Alexander Graham Bell said that newspaper reports about his locating the bullet in Garfield's body were false because the doctors released an incorrect announcement.

Although the Garfield assassination occurred in 1881, aspects of the event seem familiar today. Like Charles Guiteau, individuals are still driven to harm public officials by their personal ambition, mental illness, politics, religious beliefs, or desire for fame.

The extensive news coverage of Garfield's suffering and death was limited to print (the only media available then). Yet it rivals the nonstop reporting of major incidents we now see and hear on our televisions, cell phones, computer screens, and radios.

Medical fiascoes—the results of ignorance, arrogance, and carelessness—still occur. Fortunately, advances in knowledge and technology have greatly improved medical treatment since Garfield's shooting. But when it comes to the human body, there will always be more mysteries to solve and challenges to overcome.

—GJ

ACKNOWLEDGMENTS

As I researched and wrote *AMBUSHED!*, several generous people shared their knowledge and time with me. Many thanks to Dr. Jon Willen, infectious disease specialist and expert on nineteenth-century medicine, for clarifying the medical aspects of Garfield's case, suggesting additional resources, and giving me helpful feedback on the manuscript; the James A. Garfield National Historic Site, for providing valuable material about all aspects of Garfield's life and death; Joan Kapsch of the National Park Service for answering my questions about the Garfields; Brian Spatola, of the National Museum of Health and Medicine, for filling in details about the body parts of Garfield and Guiteau stored in the museum's Anatomical Collection; Jake Wynn, of the National Museum of Civil War Medicine, for elucidating the connection between the Garfield assassination and the practice of medicine during the Civil War; and the staff of Cornell University Library for assisting me in obtaining research materials.

I'm grateful to the Calkins Creek/Boyds Mills & Kane team for their careful and inspired work during the publication process. Special thanks go to my exceptional editor, Carolyn P. Yoder, for her sound advice, sharp eye, and encouraging words.

—GJ

Part of a monument that welcomes visitors to the
James A. Garfield National Historic Site in Mentor, Ohio

Without cameras to record Garfield's assassination, illustrations were based on eyewitness accounts. This appeared in a history book written about ten years afterward. (left to right: Guiteau, Garfield, Blaine)

SOURCE NOTES

The source of each quotation in this book is found below. The citation indicates the first words of the quotation and its document source. The sources are listed either in the bibliography or below.

The following abbreviations are used:
BULL: "Official Bulletins of the President's Case," *Boston Medical and Surgical Journal*
DIARY: James A. Garfield, *The Diary of James A. Garfield*
LETTERS: John Shaw, ed., *Crete and James: Personal Letters of Lucretia and James Garfield*
PAPERS: James A. Garfield, Papers, Library of Congress
TRIAL: *Report of the Proceedings in the Case of the United States vs. Charles J. Guiteau*

CHAPTER TWO
LOG CABIN BOY (p. 10)

"There is one country . . .": Hinsdale, p. 8.

"hunger and thirst . . .": DIARY, May 15, 1874, vol. 2, p. 323.

"was never still . . .": Eliza Garfield in family history, February 14, 1869, PAPERS, series 17, subseries 17D.

"Punished S. Herrington . . .": DIARY, November 13, 1849, vol. 1, p. 28.

"By the providence . . .": DIARY, October 1, 1850, vol. 1, p. 60.

"If I am blessed . . .": DIARY, July 22, 1854, vol. 1, p. 268.

"There are 25000 books. . . .": letter from Garfield to his mother, August 22, 1854, PAPERS, series 2.

"One of the greatest . . ." and "His massive figure . . .": S. G. W. Benjamin, *The Life and Adventures of a Free Lance: Being the Observations of S. G. W. Benjamin, Late United States Minister to Persia, Author, Artist and Journalist*, Burlington, VT: Free Press, 1914, p. 142.

"I have for some years . . .": DIARY, August 22, 1859, vol. 1, p. 340.

"Slavery has had its . . .": DIARY, October 22, 1857, vol. 1, p. 298.

"I can see nothing . . ." and "to stand by the country . . .": letter from Garfield to Crete, April 14, 1861, LETTERS, p. 113.

"No one who sees the splendor . . .": letter from Garfield to Crete, June 14, 1862, LETTERS, p. 142.

"The President's head . . .": letter from Garfield to Crete, September 27, 1862, LETTERS, p. 159.

"This fighting . . .": letter from Garfield to Crete, March 10, 1862, LETTERS, p. 130.

"I still struggle . . .": letter from Garfield to Crete, December, 13, 1863, LETTERS, p. 195.

"I lament sorely . . .": letter from Garfield to J. H. Rhodes, November 19, 1862, pp. 1–2, PAPERS, series 5.

"Poverty is very . . .": letter from Garfield to Board of Trustees, Geauga Seminary, May 8 1867, quoted in Fuller, p. 3.

"It is a pity . . .": DIARY, May 28, 1873, vol. 2, p. 186.

"Do you know . . .": letter from Garfield to Mollie, June 17, 1870, PAPERS, series 21.

"I did not know . . .": DIARY, October 27, 1876, vol. 3, p. 371.

CHAPTER THREE
A DARK HORSE (p. 26)

"He had in him . . .": "The Republican Candidates," *Harper's Weekly*, June 26, 1880.

"This body of slavery . . .": "The Constitutional Amendment Abolishing Slavery," January 13, 1865, in Garfield, *The Works of James Abram Garfield*, vol. 1, p. 74.

"My heart is so broken . . .": letter from Garfield to Crete, April 17, 1865, LETTERS, p. 218.

"The rush for office . . .": letter from Garfield to Captain Plumb, March 27, 1869, quoted in Theodore Clarke Smith, vol. 1, p. 446.

"thousands of men and women . . .": "Garfield Nominated," *Washington Post*, June 9, 1880.

"I would rather be with you . . .": quoted in Stanley-Brown.

"Now, that we have made . . .": quoted in *Harper's Weekly*, October 23, 1880, p. 685.

"a life of increasing . . .": quoted by Thomas Garfield in "'Recollections of the Life of James A. Garfield,' dictated by his brother, Thomas Garfield, circa 1882," PAPERS, series 21.

"I close the year . . .": DIARY, December 31, 1880, vol. 4, p. 519.

CHAPTER FOUR
THE LONER (p. 41)

"I thought he was a fool . . .": John Guiteau, TRIAL, p. 486.

"much evidence of . . .": letter from Jonathan Burt to Luther Guiteau,
    March 24, 1865, quoted in Clark, p. 6.

"Don't you think I would . . .": quoted in Dunmire, p. 90.

"I presume no one ever. . . .": Dunmire, p. 75.

"It was impossible . . .": Dunmire, p. 114.

"should be President . . .": Guiteau, TRIAL, p. 603.

"They seemed to be highly . . .": Guiteau, "Autobiography of Charles Julius
    Guiteau," p. 36.

"I had ideas . . .": same as above.

CHAPTER FIVE
THE VOW (p. 50)

"I must confront . . .": DIARY, December 11, 1880, vol. 4, p. 505.

"To-night I am a private . . .": "The World's Wrath," Class Dinner, March 3, 1881
    in Garfield, Garfield's Words, p. 135.

"that the Union was preserved . . .": "Inaugural address," p. 7, PAPERS, series 21.

"colored persons": 1880 United States Census.

"comes to its inheritance . . .": "Inaugural address," p. 6

"The crowd of callers . . .": DIARY, March 5, 1881, vol. 4, p. 553.

"Almost every one who comes . . .": DIARY, December 11, 1880, vol. 4, p. 505.

"These people are merciless; . . .": quoted in Joseph Stanley-Brown.

"Mr. Guiteau, the President . . .": quoted by Guiteau, in TRIAL, November 30,
    1881, p. 589.

"kept coming repeatedly:" Joseph Stanley Brown, TRIAL, p. 208.

"he should be quietly . . .": same as above, p. 209.

"I think I have a right . . .": letter Guiteau to James Blaine, March 11, 1881,
    in TRIAL, p. 124.

"I had every reason to expect . . .": Guiteau, "Autobiography of Charles Julius
    Guiteau," pp. 37-38.

"for intelligence . . .": James Blaine, TRIAL, p. 132.

"no prospect whatever . . .": same as above, p. 123.

"gave me a feeling . . .": DIARY, April 15, 1881, vol. 4, p. 576.

"The war of Conkling . . .": DIARY, May 20, 1881, vol. 4, p. 597.

"greatly perplexed . . .": Guiteau, TRIAL, p. 593.

"I have been trying . . .": letter Guiteau to Garfield, May 23, 1881, TRIAL, p. 212.

"an impression came over . . .": Guiteau, Trial, p. 593.

"it kept growing . . .": same as above.

"wrecked the once grand . . .": letter Guiteau to the American people,
    June 16, 1881, TRIAL, p. 216.

CHAPTER SIX

STALKING (p. 60)

"My God! What . . .": quoted in Hamilton, p. 514.

"I have been dealing all . . .": same as above.

"My anxiety for her . . .": DIARY, May 8, 1881, vol. 4, p. 588.

"The dear one is . . .": DIARY, June 9, 1881, vol. 4, p. 607.

"a very stupid sermon": DIARY, June 12, 1881, vol. 4, p. 609.

"would certainly shoot him": Guiteau, "Autobiography of Charles Julius
    Guiteau," p. 44.

"proved a traitor . . ." and "This is not murder . . .": letter from Guiteau to the
    American people, June 16, 1881, TRIAL, p. 216.

"destiny . . . to obey . . .": Guiteau, TRIAL, p. 671.

"Mrs. Garfield looked . . .": letter Guiteau, June 18, 1881, TRIAL, p. 216.

"Assassination can no more . . .": letter from Garfield to Hon. John Sherman,
    November 16, 1880 in *John Sherman's Recollections of Forty Years in the House,
    Senate and Cabinet: An Autobiography*, vol. 2. Chicago: Werner, 1895, p. 789.

"I felt tired . . .": Guiteau, TRIAL, p. 698.

CHAPTER SEVEN

RENDEZVOUS WITH HISTORY (p. 70)

"I had no ill-will . . .": letter from Guiteau to the White House, July 2, 1881,
    in TRIAL, pp. 215.

"a political necessity" and "I expect President Arthur . . .": letter from
    Guiteau to the American people, June 16, 1881, TRIAL, p. 216.

"the President's tragic death . . ." and "I am going to the jail": letter from
    Guiteau to the White House, July 2, 1881, in TRIAL, pp. 215-16.

"I have just shot . . .": note from Guiteau to General Sherman, TRIAL, p. 217.

"felt well in body and mind.": Guiteau, "Autobiography of Charles Julius
    Guiteau," p. 51.

"I will be out . . .": quoted by Aquilla Barton, in TRIAL, p. 198.

"working myself . . .": Guiteau, "Autobiography of Charles Julius Guiteau,"
    p. 53–54.

"You have had your . . .": quoted in Stanley-Brown.

"How much time . . .": quoted by Patrick Kearney in TRIAL, p. 186.

"there might be . . .": James Blaine, TRIAL, p. 121.

"My God! . . .": quoted by James Blaine, in TRIAL, p. 121.

"LYNCH HIM!": crowd, quoted by William Crawford, in TRIAL, p. 176.

"This is the man . . .": quoted by John Scott, in TRIAL, p. 176.

"We have got him . . .": quoted by James Blaine, in TRIAL, p. 121.

"I want this letter delivered . . .": quoted by Everett Foss, TRIAL, p. 390.

"Lynch him!" quoted by William Crawford, TRIAL, p. 176.

"I did it, and will . . .": quoted by Patrick Kearney, TRIAL, p. 187.

"I was frightened . . .": Diary of Jim Garfield, July 2, 1881, quoted in Feis, 81.

"Doctor, I am a dead man.": quoted by Smith Townshend, in letter to
  Ralph Walsh, October 12, 1881, in Walsh and McArdle, p. 624.

CHAPTER EIGHT

IN SHOCK (p. 81)

"In many cases, . . .": S. D. Gross, *A Manual of Military Surgery; or, Hints on the
  Emergencies of Field, Camp and Hospital Practice*," Philadelphia:
  J. B. Lippincott, 1861, p. 70.

"The finger is . . .": J. Julian Chisolm, *A Manual of Military Surgery, for the
  Use of Surgeons in the Confederate Army*, Charleston: Evans & Cogswell,
  1861, p. 122.

"The President wishes me . . .": quoted in "The President's Dispatch to
  Mrs. Garfield", *Washington Evening Star*, July 2, 1881.

"THE PRESIDENT IS SHOT!": policeman quoted in "The Shooting
  Described," *New York Sun*, July 3 1881.

"The President is shot! . . .": same as above.

"the coolest man . . .": letter from Lincoln to Norman Williams, July 28, 1881,
  quoted in Emerson, p. 228.

"that the President is assassinated.": quoted by Harriet Blaine, in letter to
  M.[daughter Margaret], July 3, 1881, in Blaine, p. 210.

"Whatever happens . . .": same as above, p. 211.

"I am home and. . . .": quoted by Edson, p. 612.

"His greatest anxiety . . .": Edson, p. 613.

"Why did he . . .": quoted by Edson, p. 613.

"You stick to me . . .": . quoted in "A Great Nation in Grief," *New York Times*,
  July 3, 1881.

"I wish I had given . . .": quoted by James Brooks, TRIAL, p. 1729.

"Garfield Shot Twice . . .": *Las Vegas Daily Gazette*, July 3, 1881.

"A Cry of Horror . . .": *Chicago Tribune*, July 3, 1881.

"His Life Hangs . . .": *Sunday Globe* [St Paul, MN], July 3, 1881.

"all hope was given up." and "Papa was expected . . .": Jim Garfield, Diary, July 2, 1881, quoted in Feis, pp. 81–82.

"very brave . . .": same as above, p. 82.

"We are so glad . . .": quoted by Edson, p. 613.

"You are a brave . . .": same as above.

"The upper story . . ." and "keep up . . .": Jim Garfield, Diary, July 2, 1881, quoted in Feis, p. 82.

"absolute quiet." Bliss, TRIAL, p. 241.

CHAPTER NINE

UNCERTAINTY (p. 92)

"If I can't save . . .": quoted in "Doctors Disagreeing," *Chicago Tribune*, July 4, 1881.

"Your injury . . ." and "Well, Doctor, we'll take . . .": quoted by Bliss, "The Story of President Garfield's Illness," p. 300.

"I am afraid . . .": unidentified doctor quoted in "Doctors Disagreeing," *Chicago Tribune*, July 4, 1881.

"was bad at the start": quoted in Lodge, p. 492.

"neither the President . . .": same as above, p. 494.

"friend Arthur President.": letter Guiteau to the American people, June 16, 1881, TRIAL, p. 216.

"narrow and bitter . . ." and "His [Guiteau's] resentment . . .": "The Assassination," *New York Times*, July 3, 1881.

"Arthur for President! . . .": Diary, July 3, 1881, in Rutherford Birchard Hayes, p. 23.

"that again has violence . . .": The [Richmond, VA] *Whig*, July 2, 1881, quoted in "Richmond Press Opinion," *Hartford* [CT] *Courant*, July 3, 1881.

"There will in all the earth . . .": "The Attempt to Kill the President," *Richmond Dispatch*, July 3, 1881.

"How is our President . . .": telegram from W. C. Pippett to Executive Mansion, July 4, 1881, PAPERS, series 4, vol. 145.

"My thanks to kind . . .": letter from Geo. E. King to President, July 2, 1881, PAPERS, same as above.

"Stick to it . . .": note from Wm. A. Kasson to Garfield, July 3, 1881, PAPERS, same as above.

"Should the President die . . .": telegram from Fred. K. Schwatka LT USA to

General W. Sherman, July 2, 1881, PAPERS, same as above.

"I guess your papa . . ." and "Oh yes . . .": quoted by Edson, p. 617.

"a wretch . . ." and "a disappointed office-seeker . . ." and "was obviously . . .":
    "The Assassination," *New York Times*, July 3, 1881.

"a pale, emaciated . . .": "The Assassin's Tale," *Evening Critic* [Washington, DC],
    July 2, 1881.

"for the hot southern . . .": "The Attempt to Kill the President," *Richmond* [VA]
    Dispatch, July 3, 1881.

CHAPTER TEN
"THE NATION'S PATIENT" (p. 108)

"THE NATION'S PATIENT": *New York Herald*, July 19, 1881.

"There never was a little girl . . .": letter from Kate Sprague to Garfield,
    July 6, 1881, PAPERS, series 4.

"healthy pus": Official Bulletin, July 11, 1881, 1:00 p.m., in Reyburn, p. 30.

"Isn't it time . . .": quoted in Rockwell, p. 437.

"Oh, it's healing splendidly . . .": quoted in "The President's Wounds," *New York
    Times*, July 9, 1881.

"That is good, but . . .": same as above.

"I should think the people . . .": quoted in Theodore Clarke Smith, p. 1191.

"The whole country seemed. . . ..": "The President," *Harper's Weekly*,
    July 23, 1881, p. 482.

"self-sacrificing wife": "Women of the Hour," *Indianapolis* [IN] *Leader*,
    July 23, 1881.

"Yours until death . . .": "Satan's Compliments," *Evening Star* [Washington, DC],
    August 18, 1881.

"The President has passed . . .": BULL, July 16, 1881, 7:00 p.m., p. 302.

"the progress of the President . . .": BULL, July 20, 1881, 8:30 a.m., p. 302.

"she considered . . .": quoted in letter from Harriet Blaine to M., July 22, 1881,
    in Blaine, p. 221.

JOSEPH LISTER'S WAR ON INFECTION (p. 120)

"was not so thoroughly . . .": Reyburn, p. 25.

CHAPTER ELEVEN
THE CHANNEL OF PUS (p. 124)

"You must keep up . . .": letter from Willie Reinig to Garfield, August 3, 1881, PAPERS, series 4.

"Very well; . . .": Bliss, p. 301.

"His face is very pale . . .": letter from Alexander Graham Bell to Mabel Hubbard Bell, July 26, 1881, Alexander Graham Bell Family Papers, 1834–1974, Manuscript Division, Library of Congress.

"These bulletins were often . . .": Reyburn, p. 19.

"Rumors concerning unfavorable . . .": telegram from Brown to Alexander Graham Bell, August 8, 1881, PAPERS, series 6.

"Surgeons believe President . . .": telegram from Brown to T. C. Crawford, August 9, 1881, PAPERS, series 6.

"Plainly I do not see . . .": letter from Harriet Blaine to You-uns, July 31, 1881, in Blaine, p. 225.

"Papa doing gloriously; . . .": Mollie Garfield, diary, August 1, 1881, PAPERS, series 21.

"Papa doing splendidly.": Jim Garfield, diary, August 4, 1881, quoted in Feis, p. 90.

"a general feeling of anxiety . . .": "On the Brink," *St. Paul* [MN] *Daily Globe*, August 17, 1881.

"the wound looks better . . .": quoted in "Dr. Bliss Reassured," *New York Times*, August 17, 1881.

"somewhat restless": BULL, August 16, 1881, 8:30 a.m., p. 306.

"tranquil": BULL, August 16, 1881, 12:30 p.m., p. 307.

"Party difference has disappeared . . .": "The President," *Harper's Weekly*, September 3, 1881.

"I consider that his chances . . .": quoted in "Dr. Hamilton's Cheerful View," *New York Tribune*, August 30, 1881.

"I never heard a groan . . .": Edson, p. 614.

"I am glad . . .": quoted in Reyburn, August 28, 1881, p. 73.

"I want to get away": quoted by Reyburn, August 24, 1881, p. 68.

CHAPTER TWELVE
ELBERON (p. 139)

"I have always felt that the ocean . . .": DIARY, June 19, 1881, vol. 4, p. 613.

"Poor dear Gaffy, how wretched . . .": letter from Harriet Blaine to M.,
    September 1, 1881, in Blaine, p. 235.

"Well, is this the last day . . ." and "No, no . . ." : quoted in Reyburn,
    September 5, 1881, p. 80.

"I do not care to go." Jim Garfield, diary, September 5, quoted in Feis, p. 91.

"The President has been . . .": quoted in "What the Doctors Say" *New York Times*,
    September 7, 1881.

"It was perfectly apparent . . .": Reyburn, p. 86.

"He is just . . .": letter Harriet Blaine to Dearest Children, September 8, 1881,
    in Blaine, p. 239.

"His general condition . . .": BULL, September 8, 1881, 8:00 a.m., p. 325.

"he was himself again": quoted in Reyburn, p. 90.

"Why, the child . . .": quoted in Feis, p. 93.

"I intended to kill . . .": quoted by Captain John McGilvray in "Guiteau Shot
    At," *National Republican*, September 12, 1881.

"had shot a good...": "Guiteau Shot At," same as above.

"This is delightful; it is . . .": quoted in Reyburn, p. 89.

"He has certainly not . . .": BULL, September 15, 1881, 9:00 a.m., p. 326.

"The President may live . . .": quoted in Adams, p. 248.

"Doctor, am I not . . ." and "Your condition is critical" and "I thought so.": quoted
    in Reyburn, p. 93.

"Do you think my name . . ." and "Yes, a grand one, . . ." and "No, my work is
    done.": quoted in Reyburn, p. 94.

"Oh my! Swaim . . ." quoted in Reyburn, p. 95.

"Oh! What is the matter?" quoted in Bliss, p. 304.

"Mrs. Garfield . . .": Bliss, p. 304.

CHAPTER THIRTEEN
THE RETURN HOME (p. 152)

"The whole period was . . .": Stanley-Brown.

"We all thought darling . . .": Mollie Garfield, Diary, September 29, 1881,
    PAPERS, series 21.

"The President Dead. PASSING . . .": *Washington Post*, September 20, 1881.

"DEAD. The Long . . .": *Sacramento [CA] Daily Record-Union*, September 20, 1881.

"The President's death . . .": "The Dead President," *New York Tribune*,
    September 20, 1881.

"the bitter disappointment . . .": "President Garfield," *Harper's Weekly*,
    September 24, 1881.

"Perhaps its most important . . .": letter Hayes to Emile Kahn, October 1, 1881,
    in Rutherford Birchard Hayes, vol. 4, p. 37.

"shrunken and emaciated features." "Looking Upon the Dead," *New York Times*,
    September 23, 1881.

CHAPTER FOURTEEN
THE MISSING BULLET (p. 162)

"We made a mistake.": quoted in Stanley-Brown.

"Gentlemen . . .": same as above.

"no different course . . .": Reyburn, p. 107.

"could only result . . .": same as above, p. 97.

"'IGNORANCE IS BLISS'": quoted in "Exchange Scintillations," *South Kentuckian*,
    August 30, 1881.

"The people of the United States . . .": same as above.

"A very valuable . . .": Hunt, p. 506.

"The fact that the president . . .": "The Doctors' Quarrel," *St. Paul* [MN]
    Daily Globe, September 24, 1881.

CHAPTER FIFTEEN
THE TRIAL (p. 170)

"We say that his death . . .": Guiteau, TRIAL, p. 264.

"I suspect I am wicked . . .": Mollie Garfield, Diary, September 29, 1881,
    PAPERS, series 21.

"as dreadful a villain . . ." and "the most interesting . . .": letter from Harriet
    Blaine to M., December 11, 1881, in Blaine, pp. 260–61.

"Guiteau never had . . .": Scoville, TRIAL, p. 286.

"I will ask you . . .": Corkhill, TRIAL, pp. 1165-66.

"I never did.": Annie Dunmire, TRIAL, p. 1166.

"I was doing the work . . .": Guiteau, TRIAL, p. 663.

"I was the only man . . .": Guiteau, TRIAL, p. 661.

"to remove the President . . ." and "intended to execute . . ." and "I think the doctors . . .": Guiteau, TRIAL, p. 616.

"I deny the killing . . .": Guiteau, TRIAL, p. 226.

"If you should think that the prisoner . . .": Judge Cox, TRIAL, p. 2348.

"Gentlemen of the jury . . .": clerk, TRIAL, p. 2348.

"We have.": John Hamlin, TRIAL, p. 2348.

"What say you? . . .": clerk, TRIAL, p. 2348.

"Guilty as indicted, sir.": Hamlin, TRIAL, p. 2349.

"Guilty.": jurors, TRIAL, p. 2349.

"My blood be on . . .": Guiteau, TRIAL, p. 2349.

"be hung by the neck . . .": Judge Cox, TRIAL, p. 2421.

"God Almighty will curse . . .": Guiteau, TRIAL, p. 2421.

"I have but one . . .": letter from Harriet Blaine to M., January 25, 1882, in Blaine, p. 291.

"Arthur, the President, is . . .": quoted in "The Execution," *Evening Star* [Washington, DC], June 30, 1882.

"Glory Hallelujah! I am going . . .": quoted in "End of Guiteau," *Evening Star* [Washington, DC], June 30, 1882.

"Glory, glory, glory!": quoted in "The Execution of Guiteau," *Evening Star* [Washington, DC], July 1, 1882.

CHAPTER SIXTEEN
THE REST OF THE STORY (p. 184)

"It seems so so cruel to think . . .": Mollie Garfield, Diary, November 20, 1882, PAPERS, series 21.

"The North, the South . . .": T. De Witt Talmage, "The Christian Statesman, James A. Garfield," *Frank Leslie's Sunday Magazine*, December 1881, p. 579.

BIBLIOGRAPHY

*Indicates primary sources

Ackerman, Kenneth D. *Dark Horse: The Surprise Election and Political Murder of President James A. Garfield*. New York: Carroll & Graf, 2003.

Adams, J. Howe. *History of the Life of D. Hayes Agnew, M.D., LL.D.* Philadelphia: F. A. Davis Company, 1892.

*Agnew, D. Hayes. *The Principles and Practice of Surgery, Being a Treatise on Surgical Diseases and Injuries*. Vol. 1. Philadelphia: J. B. Lippincott, 1878.

American Experience: Murder of a President. Directed by Rob Rapley. PBS and WGBH Educational Foundation, 2016.

*Baker, Frank. "President Garfield's Case: A Diagnosis Made July 4th." *Walsh's Retrospective*, 2: 617–22.

Balch, William Ralston. *The Life of James Abram Garfield: The Complete Record of a Wonderful Career, Which, by Native Energy and Untiring Industry, Led Its Hero from Obscurity to the Foremost Position in the American Nation*. Philadelphia: Hubbard Bros, 1881.

*Bell, Alexander Graham. "Upon the Electrical Experiments to Determine the Location of the Bullet in the Body of the Late President Garfield; and Upon a Successful Form of Induction Balance for the Painless Detection of Metallic Masses in the Human Body." *Proceedings of the American Association for the Advancement of Science, Thirty-First Meeting, August 1882*. Salem, MA: Salem Press, 1883. pp.151–206.

*Blaine, Mrs. James G. *Letters of Mrs. James G. Blaine*. Vol. 1. Edited by Harriet S. Blaine Beale. New York: Duffield and Company, 1908.

*Bliss, D. W. "The Story of President Garfield's Illness, Told by the Physician in Charge." *Century Illustrated Monthly Magazine*, Vol. 23 (December 1881): 299–305.

Bowman, Winston. *United States v. Guiteau: Assassination and Insanity in Gilded Age America*. Washington, DC: Federal Judicial Center, 2019.

Bundy, J. M. *The Life of James Abram Garfield, Twentieth President of the United States: With an Account of the President's Death and Funeral Obsequies*. New York: A. S. Barnes, 1881.

Clark, James C. *The Murder of James A. Garfield: The President's Last Days and the Trial and Execution of His Assassin*. Jefferson, NC: McFarland, 1993.

Comer, Lucretia Garfield. *Harry Garfield's First Forty Years: A Man of Action in a Troubled World*. New York: Vantage Press, 1965.

*Dunmire, Annie J. "Married Life of Charles Julius Guiteau." In *A Complete History of the Trial of Charles Julius Guiteau, Assassin of President Garfield* by H. G. and C. J. Hayes, pp. 67-137. Philadelphia: Hubbard Bros, 1882.

*Edson, C. A. "The Sickness and Nursing of President Garfield with Many Interesting Incidents Never Before Given to the Public." In *The Life of James Abram Garfield* by William Ralston Balch, pp. 612-20. Philadelphia: Hubbard Bros, 1881.

Eltorai, Ibfrahim M. "Fatal Spinal Cord Injury of the 20th President of the United States: Day-By-Day Review of his Clinical Course with Comments." *Journal of Spinal Cord Medicine*, 2004: 330–41.

Emerson, Jason. *Giant in the Shadows: The Life of Robert T. Lincoln*. Carbondale, IL: Southern Illinois University Press, 2012.

Esmarch, Friedrich. "Concerning the Treatment of the Wound of President Garfield. *Boston Medical and Surgical Journal*, Vol. 107 (September 7, 1882): 234–37.

Fcis, Ruth S-B. *Mollie Garfield in the White House*. Chicago: Rand McNally, 1963.

Fish, Stewart A. "The Death of President Garfield." *Bulletin of the History of Medicine*, Vol. 24 (1950): 378–92.

Fitzharris, Lindsey. *The Butchering Art: Joseph Lister's Quest to Transform the Grisly World of Victorian Medicine*. New York: Scientific American / Farrar, Straus and Giroux, 2017.

*Fuller, Corydon E. *Reminiscences of James A. Garfield with Notes Preliminary and Collateral*. Cincinnati, OH: Standard Publishing, 1887.

*Garfield, James A. *The Diary of James A. Garfield*. Vols. 1–4. Edited by Harry James Brown and Frederick D. Williams. East Lansing, MI: Michigan State University Press, 1967–1981.

*_____. *Garfield's Words: Suggestive Passages from the Public and Private Writings of James Abram Garfield*. Compiled by William Ralston Balch. Boston: Houghton Mifflin, 1881.

*_____. "My Experience as a Lawyer." *North American Review*, Vol. 144 (1887): 565–71.

*_____. Papers. Manuscript/Mixed Material, Library of Congress, Washington, DC.

*_____. *The Works of James Abram Garfield*, Vols. 1 and 2. Edited by B. A. Hinsdale. Boston: James R. Osgood, 1882 and 1883.

James A. Garfield National Historic Site. Mentor, Ohio.

*Guiteau, Charles. *The Truth and the Removal*. Washington, DC, 1882.

*Guiteau, Charles Julius. "Autobiography of Charles Julius Guiteau, Assassin of President Garfield." In *A Complete History of the Trial of Charles Julius Guiteau, Assassin of President Garfield* by H. G. and C. J. Hayes, pp. 17–66. Philadelphia: Hubbard Bros, 1882.

Hamilton, Gail. *Biography of James G. Blaine*. Norwich, CT: Henry Bill Publishing, 1895.

Hayes, H. G. and C. J. Hayes. *A Complete History of the Trial of Charles Julius Guiteau, Assassin of President Garfield*. Philadelphia: Hubbard Bros, 1882.

*Hayes, Rutherford Birchard. *Diary and Letters of Rutherford Birchard Hayes. Nineteenth President of the United States*. Vol. 4. Edited by Charles Richard Williams. Columbus, OH: Ohio State Archaeological and Historical Society, 1925.

Herr, Harry W. "Ignorance Is Bliss: The Listerian Revolution and Education of American Surgeons." *Journal of Urology*, Vol. 177 (February 2007): 457–60.

Hinsdale, B. A. *The Republican Text-Book for the Campaign of 1880: A Full History of General James A. Garfield's Public Life, With Other Political Information*. New York: D. Appleton, 1880.

Hunt, William. "Dr. William Hunt on President Garfield's Case." *Boston Medical and Surgical Journal*, 105 (November 24, 1881): 505–07.

Kirke, Edmund [Gilmore, James R.]. *The Life of James A. Garfield, President of the United States*. New York: Harper, 1880.

*Lamb, D. S. "Report of the Post-Mortem Examination of the Body of Charles J. Guiteau." *Medical News*, Vol. 41 (July 8, 1882): 43–45.

Life Portrait of James Garfield. American Presidents Series. C-Span, July 26, 1999.

*Lister, Joseph. "The Antiseptic Method of Dressing Open Wounds: A Clinical Lecture." *Medical Record*, Vol. 11 (October 21, 1876): 695–96.

*_____."Antiseptic Surgery." *Transactions of the International Medical Congress of Philadelphia*, 1876: 535–44.

Lodge, E. A., Sr. "President Garfield's Case: Dr. Boynton's Statement." *American Observer Medical Monthly*, November 1881: 492–503.

Millard, Candice. *Destiny of the Republic: A Tale of Madness, Medicine and the Murder of a President*. New York: Anchor Books, 2011.

Miller, Joseph M. "The Death of James Abram Garfield." *Surgery, Gynecology, and Obstetrics*, Vol. 107 (July 1958): 113–18.

Mitchell, Stewart. "The Man Who Murdered Garfield." *Massachusetts Historical Society, Proceedings 1941–1944*, Vol. 67 : 452–89.

*"Official Bulletins of the President's Case." *Boston Medical and Surgical Journal*. Vol. 105 (September 29, 1881): 299–307 and (October 6, 1881): 322-30.

Pappas, Theodore N., and Shahrzad Joharifard. "Did James A. Garfield Die of Cholecystitis? Revisiting the Autopsy of the 20th President of the United States." *American Journal of Surgery*, Vol. 206 (October 2013): 614–17.

Paulson, George "Death of a President and his Assassin: Errors in their Diagnosis and Autopsies." *Journal of the History of the Neurosciences*, Vol. 15 (2006): 77–91.

Peskin, Allan. *Garfield: A Biography*. Kent, OH: Kent State University Press, 1978.

Prichard, Robert W., and A. L. Herring, Jr. "The Problem of the President's Bullet." *Surgery, Gynecology, and Obstetrics*, Vol. 92 (May 1951): 625–33.

Report of the Proceedings in the Case of the United States vs. Charles J. Guiteau, Tried in the Supreme Court of the District of Columbia, Holding a Criminal Term, and Beginning November 14, 1881. Parts 1, 2, and 3. Washington, DC: Government Printing Office, 1882.

*Reyburn, Robert. *Clinical History of the Case of President James Abram Garfield*. Chicago: Journal of the American Medical Association, 1894.

Riddle, A. G. *The Life, Character and Public Services of Jas. A. Garfield*. Cleveland, OH: W. W. Williams, 1881.

Ridpath, John Clark. *The Life and Work of James A. Garfield, Twentieth President of the United States*. Memorial Edition. Cincinnati, OH: Jones Brothers, 1881.

Robertson, Archie. "'Murder Most Foul.'" *American Heritage*, Vol. 15 (August 1964): 90–104.

*Rockwell, Almon. "From Mentor to Elberon." *Century Illustrated Monthly Magazine*, Vol. 23 (January 1882): 431–38.

Rosenberg, Charles E. *The Trial of the Assassin Guiteau: Psychiatry and Law in the Gilded Age*. Chicago, IL: University of Chicago Press, 1968.

Rutkow, Ira. *James A. Garfield*. New York: Henry Holt, 2006.

_____. *Seeking the Cure: A History of Medicine in America*. New York: Scribner, 2010.

Schwarz, Frederic D. "1881, President Garfield Shot." *American Heritage*, Vol. 57 (June/July 2006): 72.

Seale, William. *The President's House: A History*. Vol. 1. 2nd Edition. Baltimore, MD: Johns Hopkins University Press, 2008.

*Shaw, John, ed. *Crete and James: Personal Letters of Lucretia and James Garfield*. East Lansing, MI: Michigan State University Press, 1994.

Smith, Theodore Clarke. *The Life and Letters of James Abram Garfield*. Vols. 1 and 2. New Haven, CT: Yale University Press, 1925.

Smith, T. Burton. "Assassination Medicine." *American Heritage*, Vol. 43 (September 1992): 116–19.

*Stanley-Brown, Joseph. "My Friend Garfield." *American Heritage*, Vol. 22 (August 1971).

Tempkin, Owsei, and Janet Koudelka. "Simon Newcomb and the Location of President Garfield's Bullet." *Bulletin of the History of Medicine*, Vol. 24 (1950): 393–97.

Turnipseed, E. B. "Dissenting Voice from the Standpoints Taken by D. W. Bliss, M.D., in Regard to the Diagnosis, Prognosis, and Treatment of the Case of President Garfield." *Medical Record*, Vol. 20 (December 3, 1881): 621–24.

*U.S. Navy Department. *Reports of Officers of the Navy on Ventilating and Cooling the Executive Mansion During the Illness of President Garfield*. Washington, DC: Government Printing Office, 1882.

Vermilya, Daniel J. *James Garfield and the Civil War: For Ohio and the Union*. Charleston, SC: History Press, 2015.

Walsh, Ralph, and Thomas E. McArdle, eds. *Walsh's Retrospect: A Quarterly Compendium of American Medicine and Surgery*. Vol. 2 (October 1881): 455-59, 542-57, 617-33.

Warren, J. Collins. "Case of President Garfield." *Boston Medical and Surgical Journal*, Vol. 105 (November 17, 1881): 463–66.

Weiner, Bradley K. "The Case of James A. Garfield: A Historical Perspective." *Spine*, Vol. 28 (May 2003): E183–86.

White, J. William. "A Review of Some of the More Important Surgical Problems of President Garfield's Case." *Medical News*, Vol. 40 (June 24, 1882): 677–83.

Young, James. A. "The President, His Assassin, and the Court-Martial of John A. Mason." *Air Force Review*, August 23, 2017.

ADDITIONAL ARTICLES FROM THESE SOURCES:

American Heritage
American Journal of the Medical Sciences
American Journal of Surgery
American Surgeon
Baltimore Sun
Boston Medical and Surgical Journal
Chicago Tribune
Clinical Anatomy
Daily Gazette [Wilmington, DE]
Evening Critic [Washington, DC]
Evening Star [Washington, DC]
Frank Leslie's Illustrated Newspaper
Harper's Weekly
Hartford [CT] *Daily Courant*
Indianapolis [IN] *Leader*
Journal of the American College of Surgeons
Journal of the American Medical Association
Knoxville [TN] *Daily Chronicle*
Las Vegas [NV] *Daily Gazette*
Medical Gazette
Medical History
Medical News
Medical Record
New York Herald
New York Sun
New York Times
New York Tribune
Omaha [NE] *Daily Bee*
Prologue
Richmond [VA] *Dispatch*
Sacramento [CA] *Daily Record-Union*
Salt Lake [UT] *Daily Herald*
Smithsonian.com
St. Paul [MN] *Daily Globe*
Washington [DC] *Post*
Wheeling [WV] *Register*

INDEX

Page numbers in **boldface** refer to images and/or captions.

FRANK LESLIE'S
ILLUSTRATED
NEWSPAPER

No. 1,846.—Vol. LII.   NEW YORK, JULY 16, 1881.   [Price 10 Cents.

WASHINGTON, D. C.—THE ATTACK ON THE PRESIDENT'S LIFE—MRS. SMITH SUPPORTING THE PRESIDENT WHILE AWAITING THE ARRIVAL OF THE AMBULANCE.—From Sketches by our Special Artist's A. Berghaus, and C. Upham.—See Page 335.

This newspaper's illustration of the assassination scene depicts one of Garfield's sons, eyes covered, standing over his father. Secretary James Blaine is on the right, and Sarah White cradles the president's head.

PICTURE CREDITS

William Ralston Balch, *The Life of James Abram Garfield*, Philadelphia: Hubbard Bros, 1881: 10 (top and bottom).
"Biographical Sketch of Dr. Daniel Smith Lamb." Reprint from *Physicians and Surgeons of America*, 1896: 162.
Chicago Tribune: July 3, 1881: 75, 88 (left); July 15, 1881: 116.
Daily Gazette [Wilmington, DE], September 20, 1881: 157 (bottom left).
Evening Star [Washington, DC]: November 3, 1880: 40 (bottom); July 2, 1881: 88 (top right), 89; November 22, 1914: 123.
Flickr: DC Public Library Commons: 80.
Harper's Weekly, October 23, 1880: 36; November 20, 1880: 41, 47; July 31, 1880: 46; November 26, 1881: 62, 173; July, 23, 1881: 100, August 13, 1881: 130; October 1, 1881: 152, 156, 159; October 8, 1881: 160; December 3, 1881: 172, 176-177, 178; December 10, 1881: 179.
H. G. Hayes and C. J. Hayes. *A Complete History of the Trial of Charles Julius Guiteau, Assassin of President Garfield*. Philadelphia: Hubbard Bros, 1882: 44, 45, 86, 180.
Historical Findings: 70, 186.
A History of Cleveland, Ohio: Biographical. Volume 2. Chicago-Cleveland: S. J. Clarke Publishing, 1910: 106 (right).
Gail Jarrow: 37, 55, 187 (top and bottom), 209.
Knoxville [TN] *Daily Chronicle*, November 4, 1880: 42.
Las Vegas [NV] *Daily Gazette*, September 20, 1881: 157 (top).
Frank Leslie's Illustrated Newspaper, July 8, 1882: 182.
Library Company of Philadelphia, Marriott C. Morris Collection: 142-143.
Library of Congress, Manuscript Division, Papers of James A. Garfield: Series 1, Diaries, April 1848: 13; July 1, 1881: 68 (right); Series 3: 33, 68 (left); Series 4: 102 (left and right), 111 (top and bottom), 112, 115; Series 17, Subseries 17Q: 25(top right); Subseries 17J: 136; Series 19, Subseries 19A, Vol. 1: 204; Series 19, Subseries 19A, Vol. 2: 14, 15, 133, 158 (bottom); Series 21: 25 (bottom right).
Library of Congress, Prints & Photographs Division: LC-USZ62-209: 6; LC-DIG-stereo-1s06116: 8; LC-USZ62-100087: 23; LC-USZ62-56429: 28; LC-USZ62-76423: 30; LC-USZ62-13021: 34; LC-USZ62-112153: 35; LC-USZ62-107253: 38; LC-USZ62-22738: 50; LC-USZ62-20851: 53; LC-USZ62-23003: 64; LC-USZ62-126423: 67; LC-USZ62-44266: 100; LC-USZC4-6402: 105; LC-USZ62-104052: 107 (left); LC-DIG-ppmsca-56207: 118; LC-USZ62-104275: 131 (left); LC-USZ62-G9-Z4-116,794-T: 131 (right); LC-USZ62-134586: 132; LC-USZ61-425: 140;

LC-USZ62-93201: 142 (top); LC-USZ6-2102: 144; LC-USZ6-2103: 146-147; LC-USZ62-124389: 149; LC-USZ62-7615: 154; LC-USZ62-121654: 158 (top); LC-DIG-ds-07197: 181; LC-USZ62-64278: 200; LC-USZ62-77908: 234. Brady-Handy Collection: LC-BH832-1109: 24; LC-BH83-1940: 25 (left); LC-BH826-1449: 31 (right); LC-USZ62-13020: 60; LC-BH826-1483: 96; LC-BH826-30278: 184. Civil War Photographs, 1861-1865: LC-B8172-2218: 20. Detroit Publishing Company: LC-D4-4415: 193. Highsmith Archive: LC-DIG-highsm-41662: 161 (left). Popular Graphic Arts: LC-USZC4-1762: 19; LC-DIG-pga-11188: 27; LC-USZC4-6109: 39; LC-DIG-pga-02118: 76-77; LC-USZ62-117223: 161 (right); LC-USZC4-12531: 194; LC-USZ62-4059: 195; LC-DIG-pga-00382: 196; LC-USZ62-103801: 199.
Mary Evans Picture Library: 121.
National Library of Medicine: 83, 92, 106 (left), 106 (second from left), 107 (second from left), 107 (second from right), 107 (right), 120.
National Museum of Health and Medicine: 106 (second from right), 165, 183 (left and right).
National Republican, July 1, 1881: 69.
New York Sun, July 3, 1881: 88 (middle).
Puck, January 12, 1881: 57; April 6, 1881: 58; July 6, 1881: 91; August 3, 1881: 124; August 10, 1881: 127; September 28, 1881: 169; October 26, 1881: 170; November 30, 1881: 174.
Robert Reyburn. *Clinical History of the Case of President James Abram Garfield*. Chicago: Journal of the American Medical Association, 1894: 166.
John Clark Ridpath. *Ridpath's History of the World*. Vol. 7. Cincinnati, OH, 1907: 210.
Sacramento [CA] *Daily Record-Union*, November 3, 1880: 40 (top).
St. Paul [MN] *Daily Globe*, August 17, 1881: 134.
Sunday Globe [St. Paul, MN], July 3, 1881: 88 (bottom right).
US National Archives and Records Administration: 525612: 31 (left); General Records of the Department of State, RG 59: 49.
Washington [DC] *Post*, July 3, 1881: 93.
Wellcome Collection: 122.
Wheeling [WV] *Register*, September 20, 1881: 157 (bottom right).
Wikimedia Commons: 43, 191; Western Reserve Historical Society: 17.

GAIL JARROW'S SELECT CALKINS CREEK TITLES

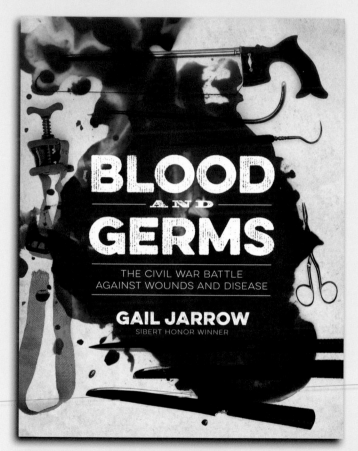

MEDICAL FIASCOES SERIES

Blood and Germs: The Civil War Battle Against Wounds and Disease

Kirkus Reviews Best Book (Middle-Grade Nonfiction)

Outstanding Science Trade Book for Students K–12—
National Science Teaching Association and Children's Book Council

CCBC Choice—Cooperative Children's Book Center

Orbis Pictus Recommended Book—National Council of Teachers of English

Best Informational Book for Older Readers—Chicago Public Library

Excellence in Nonfiction Award Nominee—Young Adult Library Services Association

Jefferson Cup for Older Readers Honor Book—Virginia Library Association

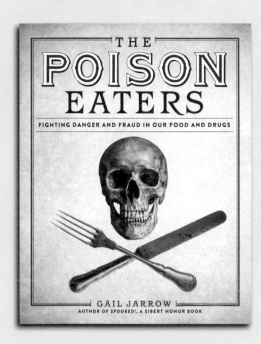

The Poison Eaters: Fighting Danger and Fraud in Our Food and Drugs

Orbis Pictus Award for Outstanding Nonfiction for Children Honor Book—National Council of Teachers of English

Notable Children's Book—Association for Library Service to Children/American Library Association

Outstanding Science Trade Book for Students—National Science Teaching Association and Children's Book Council

Notable Social Studies Trade Book for Young People—National Council for the Social Studies and Children's Book Council

Best Children's Book—Bank Street College of Education

Best Middle-Grade Book—*Kirkus Reviews*

Blue Ribbons List—*Bulletin of the Center for Children's Books*

Editors' Choice: Books for Youth—*Booklist*

Lasting Connections, Top 30—*Book Links*

Best Children's Book—*Washington Post*

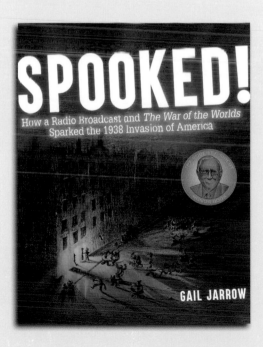

Spooked!: How a Radio Broadcast and *The War of the Worlds* Sparked the 1938 Invasion of America

Robert F. Sibert Award Honor Book—Association for Library Service to Children/American Library Association

Golden Kite Honor, Non-Fiction for Older Readers—Society of Children's Book Writers and Illustrators

Notable Children's Book—Association for Library Service to Children/American Library Association

Notable Social Studies Trade Book for Young Readers—National Council for the Social Studies and Children's Book Council

Excellence in Nonfiction Award Nominee—Young Adult Library Services Association

Quick Picks for Reluctant Young Adult Readers—Young Adult Library Services Association

Editors' Choice List—*Booklist*

Best Book—*School Library Journal*

Blue Ribbons List for Nonfiction—*Bulletin of the Center for Children's Books*

CCBC Choices Best of the Year—Cooperative Children's Book Center

Best Children's Book of the Year—Bank Street College of Education

Best Children's Book—*Washington Post*

DEADLY DISEASES TRILOGY

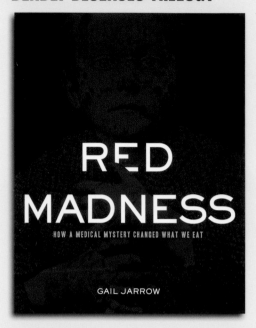

Red Madness: How a Medical Mystery Changed What We Eat

Jefferson Cup for Older Readers—Virginia Library Association

Best Book—*School Library Journal*

Best STEM Book—National Science Teaching Association and the Children's Book Council

Best Children's Book of the Year, Science—Bank Street College of Education

CCBC Choice—Cooperative Children's Book Center

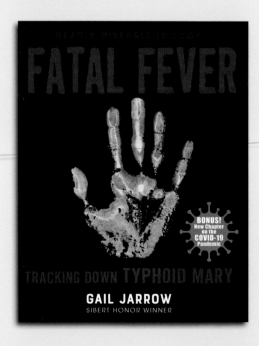

Fatal Fever: Tracking Down Typhoid Mary

Eureka! Gold Award—California Reading Association

Blue Ribbons List for Nonfiction—*Bulletin of the Center for Children's Books*

CCBC Choice—Cooperative Children's Book Center

Best Children's Book of the Year, Outstanding Merit—Bank Street College of Education

Nonfiction Honor List—VOYA

Bubonic Panic: When Plague Invaded America

Best Book—*School Library Journal*

Best Book for Teens/Best Teen Mysteries and Thrillers—*Kirkus Reviews*

Eureka! Gold Award—California Reading Association

Outstanding Science Trade Book for Students—National Science Teaching Association and the Children's Book Council

Recommended, National Science Teachers Association

Notable Social Studies Trade Book—National Council for the Social Studies and Children's Book Council

CCBC Choice—Cooperative Children's Book Center

Best Books for Teens—New York Public Library

GAIL JARROW enjoys investigating, dissecting, and analyzing little-known stories from the history of science. Her books have received many distinctions, including the YALSA Award for Excellence in Nonfiction for Young Adults; Sibert Honor Book medal; an NSTA Best STEM Book and Outstanding Science Trade Book; an ILA Best Science Book; and Orbis Pictus Honor Book. She continues her examination of diseases and infections with *Blood and Germs* and *Ambushed!* in the Medical Fiascoes series. Gail has a degree in zoology and has taught science to students of all ages. She lives in Ithaca, New York. Visit gailjarrow.com.